LEGENDS, LORE & TRUE TALES IN MORMON COUNTRY

MARK,
I BET NEITHER OF US
COULD HAVE SEEN
THIS CHAPTER COMING
BUT YOUR TRAINING
HELPED ME GET THERE.
THANKS.
, JASON

LEGENDS, LORE & TRUE TALES IN
⊰ MORMON COUNTRY ⊱

Edited by Monte Bona

CONTRIBUTIONS FROM Christian Probasco, Steven J. Clark, Eileen Hallet Stone, James Nelson, Jack C. Billings, Ed Meyer, Jack Monnett, Jason Friedman & Shirley Bahlmann

THE
History
PRESS

Published by The History Press
Charleston, SC 29403
www.historypress.net

Back bottom cover image by Barry Glazier, photographer; front top mural image (detail) by
Lynn Griffin, artist.

First published 2015

Manufactured in the United States

ISBN 978.1.62619.939.2

Library of Congress Control Number: 2015934635

CONTENTS

Introduction, by Monte Bona   7

1. San Juan Mission: Hole-in-the-Rock, by Christian Probasco   11
2. Lost Treasures of the Mormon Heritage Highway, by Steven J. Clark   25
3. Clarion: A Back-to-the-Soil Movement, by Eileen Hallet Stone   37
4. Duncan McMillan and Brigham Young, by Jason Friedman   51
5. "Names Mean Nothing": Hiram Bebee aka the Sundance Kid,
   by Jack C. Billings   61
6. Zane Grey's Ghost, by Ed Meyer   71
7. The Magical Story of Maude Adams, by James Nelson   87
8. Hans Ulrich Bryner Jr., by Jack Monnett   99
9. Frontier Justice, by Shirley Bahlmann   111

Notes   131
About the Authors   139

INTRODUCTION

Spanning 250 miles, from the small town of Fairview, Utah, southward to our border with Arizona, the area encompassed by the Mormon Pioneer National Heritage Area includes outstanding examples of historical, cultural, and natural resources shaped by Mormon pioneers. The story of the Mormon pioneers is one of the most compelling and captivating in our nation's history. After traveling 1,400 miles from Illinois either by wagon or by pulling a handcart, the pioneers came to the Great Salt Lake valley. Along the way, the pioneers experienced many hardships.... Many people died during their journey.... The Mormon Pioneer National Heritage Area will serve as special recognition to the people and places that have contributed greatly to our nation's development. Throughout the heritage area are wonderful examples of architecture...and cultural events...that demonstrate the way of life of the pioneers.
—Senator Robert F. Bennett, introduction to the
Mormon Pioneer National Heritage Act

The Mormon Pioneer National Heritage Area features breathtaking natural resources, inspiring stories and intriguing cultural traditions shaped by Mormon pioneers.

It's the story of a people who, led by faith and driven by rugged determination, braved a frontier land and carved for themselves a new home in the wilderness. It's the story of cooperation, industry, ingenuity, true grit and the occasional miracle. It's the story of the hardships and privations they endured, how they persevered through them and how they yet managed to

Picturesque landscapes along the Mormon Pioneer National Heritage Area Corridor.
Mormon Pioneer National Heritage Area.

create lives full of joy, goodness, hope and the realization of those hopes. It's the story of a people who, while heeding the call of their faith, fulfilled the Manifest Destiny call of a nation.

The experiences of the pioneer settlers provide a wealth of stories illustrative of the human spirit. Their collective and individual stories are instructive, often remarkable and almost always inspiring, given how they interacted with one another, how they interacted with the land, which was both friend and foe, and how they interacted with the Native Americans, who had a sacred connection with the land and the waters that nourish it.

The pioneers knew about synergy long before the word became popular in modern management lexicon. They had to work together in order to survive, and they had to move from conflict to cooperation with the Indians and their culture and values. They knew of the synergy created when people work together toward a common purpose. Facing obstacles and adversity, the pioneers knew they would overcome them together or not at all.

Stories require talented storytellers, and the Mormon Pioneer National Heritage Area engages the creative minds of writers. This is especially true with the authors of this work, who have also collaborated in bringing to the reader an amazing collection of stories about Sanpete County's historically rich and ethnically diverse culture, including the Jewish colonists of Clarion, the Hole-in-the-Rock settlers, a pioneering Presbyterian minister, a would-be Sundance Kid, a famous actress with Mormon pioneer roots, a legendary teller of western lore, the story of a blind pioneer, lost treasures and frontier justice. It's all here, right in the heart of Mormon country.

CHAPTER 1

SAN JUAN MISSION:
HOLE-IN-THE-ROCK

BY CHRISTIAN PROBASCO

On the southeast edge of the Mormon Pioneer National Heritage Area, near Escalante, you'll find a historical plaza commemorating a Mormon wagon train whose members chiseled and blasted a direct trail through some of the most desolate and forbidding terrain on the continent to establish a colony on the banks of the San Juan River.

Most of the saints from Parowan, Paragonah, Cedar City, Oak City and other Utah towns brought provisions to last them the six weeks they were told the trip would take. But it took them about six months to widen a narrow cleft through the stone precipice south of Escalante known as "Hole-in-the-Rock," ferry their wagons across the Colorado River and then construct roadways over more sandstone barriers in the chaotic landscape to the east to reach the land they had been called by church leaders to settle.

Local artist Lynn Griffin's murals on the walls of the Escalante/Hole-in-the-Rock Heritage Center depict those pioneers' struggles to lower their wagons to the Colorado River. In Griffin's *Last Wagon*, Arabella Smith holds back a horse tied to and anchoring the last wagon to descend the hole on the day the road was opened. Her three children watch nearby from a quilt laid over the sandstone.

Arabella's husband, Joseph Stanford Smith, would have been guiding his horse team from the seat, literally out of the picture. As the wagon slid down the slope and lurched over a boulder, the story goes, Arabella was

Lynn Griffin's *Last Wagon* depicts Arabella Smith helping to hold back the wagon driven by her husband during the dangerous descent of Hole-in-the-Rock. *Lynn Griffin.*

knocked down and then thrown against a rock wall. Although bloodied by the ordeal, she recovered and continued with her family across the Colorado River the day of their descent.[1]

Arabella and Joseph, as well as the rest of the expedition members, found themselves in this predicament because they and their leader, Silas S. Smith, had refused to give up building a shortcut through the rocky badlands of southern Utah after discovering that the task would be far more difficult than they had anticipated. Smith, of Paragonah in south-central Utah, was a cousin of the Mormon Church's founder, Joseph Smith, as well as a veteran of Utah's Black Hawk War of 1865–72 and a former member of the territorial legislature.

Smith had led an exploratory party south through the Navajo Reservation, beginning in April 1879, to a tiny new gentile settlement called "Montezuma" in the region the Mormons wanted to settle. He left two families and a few men there in May to tend to newly planted crops and improve the land above the river and then returned by an eastern route to the Spanish Trail, which took him and his crew still farther north around the forbidding rock upwarp of the San Rafael Swell and then southwest through the mountains back to their homes, which they reached in September.

By then, the main party was assembled and ready to set out. However, if they were to build shelters along the San Juan River before the coldest winter months and plant crops in the spring, following the Spanish Trail east was out of the question. That way was 450 miles. The southern route through the Navajo Reservation was also problematic. There were few waterholes along the way, and the Indian inhabitants were not interested in sharing them.

While Smith's exploratory group had been describing an arc of travel through a quarter of Utah territory, constructing and improving roads along the way, church authorities had asked residents of the newly settled

Silas S. Smith, leader of the San Juan Expedition. *Hole-in-the-Rock Foundation.*

hamlet of Escalante, about sixty miles east of Paragonah, to see if a shorter route couldn't be found through the slickrock backcountry to Montezuma.

Reuben Collett, the constable of Escalante; Andrew Schow, the town's first bishop; and Charles Hall, a cooper, reported that a narrow slot above the Colorado River, known as Hole-in-the-Rock, could be improved to accommodate wagons. Hall explained that although it would be difficult to bring wagons down to the Colorado and ferry them across, once they were on the other side "it would be a simple matter to move on to the San Juan, about sixty miles away."[2] None of the three had explored farther than the head of Cottonwood Canyon on the river's far bank.[3]

Collett and Schow visited Parowan to spread the gospel of the Hole-in-the-Rock shortcut among the gathered saints. Silas Smith, who knew Collett, Schow and Hall, made up his mind for the route in the middle of October.[4] The decision set in motion more than 230 saints, perhaps half of whom were children, and about eighty-three wagons, as well as a few hundred horses and more than one thousand cattle. The missionaries did not set out in a consolidated train but rather mostly traveled in groups strung along the often snowy trail between the desert settlements west of

Aerial view of Hole-in-the-Rock. *Lamont Crabtree.*

The Hole-in-the-Rock expedition exhibit. *Utah State Historical Society.*

the mountains and a rendezvous point at a spring forty miles south of Escalante, between the deep gulches of the Escalante River and the high edge of the Kaiparowits Plateau, known as the "Straight Cliffs."

That first camp was near "Dance Hall Rock," a smooth-floored natural stone amphitheater where the pioneers gathered to dance to fiddle music and raise their spirits for the trials ahead.

As the wagons assembled at Forty-Mile Springs, four scouts set out to reconnoiter their route. They met two prospectors returning from the badlands north of the Colorado River. According to the recollections of one scout, Kumen Jones, the prospectors warned them, "If every rag, or other property owned by the people of the territory was sold for cash, it would not pay for the making of a burro trail across the river."[5]

The scouts crossed the Colorado and hiked far enough beyond Cottonwood Canyon to see that the prospectors weren't exaggerating by much. They were on the edge of a craggy sandstone barrens stretching as far as the eye could see, dominated by the rock dome of Navajo Mountain to the south. They reported to Smith that a wagon road through the region would take weeks or months to build, if it could be constructed at all.[6]

A second scouting party of ten men, accompanied by Collett, Schow and Hall, failed to make it even as far as the first group. One scout, Platte D. Lyman, the assistant captain of the expedition, recorded in his journal:

> *The country here is almost entirely solid sand rock, high hills, and mountains all cut to pieces by deep gulches which are in many places altogether impassable. It is certainly the worst country I ever saw, some of our party are of the opinion that a road could be made if plenty of money was furnished but most of us are satisfied that there is no us*[e] *of this company undertaking to get through to San Juan this way.*[7]

Most other members of the second scouting party expressed opinions similar to Lyman's during a meeting with Silas Smith in his tent on December 3. Smith knew that it was too late to change course and pressed the case for continuing work on the road. According to Lyman, "All present expressed themselves willing to spend 3 or 4 months if necessary working on the road in order to get through, as it was almost impossible to go back the way we came because of the condition of the road and the scarcity of grass."[8]

Smith broke the news to the rest of the settlers during a camp meeting the next day. "The miracle of this decision went through the company

Cottonwood Canyon, viewed from Hole-in-the-Rock before the channel of the Colorado River filled into Lake Powell. *Lamont Crabtree.*

like an electric shock and all was good cheer and hustle," Kumen Jones recorded years later.[9] The pioneers sang "The Spirit of God Like a Fire Is Burning" and soon afterward set fervently to work improving the trail to Hole-in-the-Rock.

The terrain became rockier and more rugged as the workers neared the Colorado. As work commenced on the hole itself, another contingent of men crossed the Colorado to develop the route out of Cottonwood Canyon.

Silas Smith traveled north on December 15 to secure blasting powder and funding for the road from the territorial legislature in Salt Lake City. He left Lyman in charge. Smith expected to return in a few weeks. Although he was successful in forwarding more than one thousand pounds of powder to the expedition and securing $5,000 to partially compensate the men building the road for their efforts, he became seriously ill during his journey and did not return until the pioneers had made it through to the San Juan.

Soon after Smith left, Lyman chose four more men to scout a path all the way through the rock desert to their destination, about seventy air miles distant. The scouts set out with a pack train and eight days of provisions. They ran out of food and became lost in a blizzard but were finally able to orient themselves to the Abajo or "Blue" Mountains nearby and follow Indian trails to Montezuma.

The crops of the Mormon families at Montezuma had failed, and they were facing starvation themselves. The scouts bought some flour for the return trip from another prospector and hurried back toward the expedition, accompanied by two Mormon settlers. They became briefly lost again and ran out of food again but managed to stumble back to the Colorado River and the expedition on January 9.

With powder on the way and the certain knowledge that a route could be put through, the success of the mission boiled down to road engineering. Here the workers had an advantage, as many of them were veterans of other settlement missions and other road-building endeavors. Cornelius I. Decker, a member of the road crew, later recorded, "I don't think I ever seen a lot of men go to work with more of a will to do something than that crowd did. We were all young men; the way we did make dirt and rock fly was a caution."[10]

Among the workers at Hole-in-the-Rock were Benjamin and Hyrum Perkins, former coal miners from Wales, who knew how to use powder to its best effect. They and others were lowered down cliffs by rope to drill the rock and set charges to blast a pathway wide enough for a wagon span.

Benjamin Perkins also supervised the construction of what came to be known as "Uncle Ben's Dugway." Rather than excavate a road into a sheer wall partway down Hole-in-the-Rock, Perkins's crew cut a thin shelf for the wagons' inside wheels, pounded timbers into drill holes below the shelf and then piled logs and brush on top of the timbers to form a narrow roadway suspended above nothing.

While crews widened Hole-in-the-Rock and the route out of Cottonwood Canyon, Charles Hall hauled logs to the bank of the Colorado River and assembled them into a large raft. By the time the road was ready to receive wagons, he was ready to ferry them to the other side.

Aerial view of Hole-in-the-Rock from above Lake Powell. *Lamont Crabtree.*

Dugway constructed by pioneers in Cottonwood Canyon. *Lamont Crabtree.*

David E. Miller, author of *Hole-in-the-Rock*, a definitive work on the subject, believed it most likely that Kumen Jones made the first wheeled descent of the hole, driving Benjamin Perkins's wagon.[11] What is known for certain is that twenty-six wagons were driven down the hole the first day, January 26, and ferried across the Colorado. No wagons were seriously damaged during the process, although some of sections were so slippery that the women and children following the wagons had to sit to slide down them.

The wagons were "rough locked," meaning a chain was wrapped around the wheel rim with its ends fastened to the wagon box or rear axle to keep it at the bottom of the wheel. Other chains or ropes attached to the rear axle or box were taken up by groups of men acting as living brakes during the descent. Sometimes horses and mules were used for the same purpose, although they were often yanked off their feet and dragged down the road. Most accounts describe wagons and riders sliding down the slot in a terrifying rush, despite the rough locks and men or animals straining to hold them back.

Camps were established at the top of Cottonwood Canyon a few miles from the river while the wagons were brought across. The pioneers set out again on February 10 after workers completed a dugway up "Cottonwood Hill" across a sand slope and through another rock slot. Several wagons overturned on this leg of the journey—again, though, none was so damaged it couldn't continue.

The pioneers named their gathering place on the mesa above Cottonwood Hill "Cheese Camp." While they were parked there, men from Panguitch brought them provisions gathered from their tithing office, including 240 pounds of pork and 40 pounds of cheese. The cheese was raffled off, although the purpose of the raffle is lost to history.

The Chute, stained with streaks left by wagon rims and modern off-road vehicle tires.
Lamont Crabtree.

A conflict arose at Cheese Camp between the horse ranchers, who wanted to move their stock ahead to graze on the grass and shadscale of Grey Mesa, and the wagon train drivers, who were afraid the horses would leave nothing behind for their animals. Both factions armed themselves with rifles. Platte Lyman brokered a compromise whereby the stockmen would herd their animals across the mesa without stopping them to graze.

George Hobbs set out from Cheese Camp with another pack train to relieve the Mormons at Montezuma and save them from starvation. Meanwhile, crews continued construction through the rock fissure of Wilson Canyon and then up a seam in a near-vertical wall they called "The Chute." A few dugways beyond the Chute and the pioneers were atop level, sandy Grey Mesa, just north of the stone escarpments of the San Juan River.

It took workers a week to cut a precarious route off the mesa through the sandstone domes known as the "Slick Rocks." In a letter to her parents, Elizabeth Decker, wife of Cornelius, wrote that the Slick Rocks and landscape to the east were "the roughest country you, or anybody else ever seen; it's nothing in the world but rocks and holes, hills and hollows. The mountains are just one solid rock as smooth as an apple."[12]

The pioneers' road through the "Slick Rocks." *Lamont Crabtree.*

The trail continued northeast on a sandy flat to an unlikely lake named "Pagahrit," impounded by a splay of sand that has since been washed away. Indian ruins stood on a ledge above the lake. The pioneers washed their clothes and fixed their wagons at Pagahrit Lake, and when the way ahead was clear, they continued their trek across the dam.

Deep sand in Castle Wash slowed their progress. Beyond the wash, the men cut a road through the soft blue earth of Clay Hill Pass down one thousand feet to Whirlwind Bench. A scouting party found a route that avoided the deep, sheer-walled gorge known as Grand Gulch. The wagons descended Clay Hill Pass on March 13, in bitter cold. The work crews exchanged picks and drills for axes to hew through a forest of pinyon and juniper trees. Here they met an old Ute Indian who was incredulous that they had built a road from Escalante.

Soon they were working rock again, chopping "The Twist" through sandstone breaks to Road Canyon, which was lined with the ruins of Anasazi dwellings, and then it was on to Comb Wash. Comb Ridge, a thousand-foot-high rock wall east of Comb Wash, was the last major obstacle for the pioneers, and it was as formidable as anything they had yet encountered. The spring runoff had raised the level of the San Juan, submerging the riverbank the Mormons had hoped to follow around the ridge's south edge. This was in late March. By then, their draft

The steep, narrow pioneer trail up San Juan Hill, on the southern edge of Comb Ridge. *Lamont Crabtree.*

animals were exhausted, yet they were close to their destination. As the wagons gathered at the ridge's southern edge, the men began building a final route up an impossibly steep slope, known as "San Juan Hill," to the summit.

In early April, the first wagons started up the new road, drawn by horses seven abreast. The pioneers had to beat their animals to make progress up the incline. According to Charles Redd, son of pioneer L.H. Redd, in his account, "Short Cut to San Juan": "After several pulls, rests, and pulls, many of the horses took to spasms and near-convulsions, so exhausted were they. By the time most of the outfits were across, the worst stretches could easily be identified by the dried blood and matted hair from the forelegs of the struggling teams."[13]

The crest of the stone bulwark was even, but a steep switchback road had to be built down to Butler Wash, which they were able to cross with little difficulty. Once they were standing on dirt again, most of the pioneers decided that they had gone far enough, even though Montezuma was less than twenty miles distant. The soil just east of Butler Wash was as rich as at Montezuma and mostly unclaimed. They divided the land and built a fortified settlement they called Bluff City. As it never amounted to much more than a village, the name was shortened to Bluff.

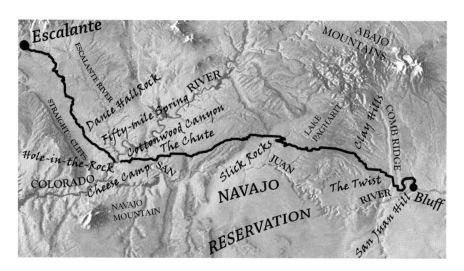

The pioneer route to their new home on the San Juan River. *Author's map.*

Two healthy babies had been born during the journey. A stillbirth may have occurred at Escalante, although the parents' identities are not known.[14] There were no other deaths recorded along the way. April 13 marked the first birth at Bluff: Morris Decker, born to Emma and Nathaniel Alvin. Roswell Stevens was recorded as the first expedition member to die at Bluff, on May 14.

The pioneers quickly set to improving the land and planting crops. But the history of Bluff by the San Juan River is like the story of a sandcastle by the sea. The river persistently demolished the settlers' dams, wrecked their canals and waterwheels and flooded their fields. In 1884, it rose to flood the town, submerge the fields and consume all the houses in Montezuma except one.

The floods of the 1880s were followed by a drought in the 1890s. Many pioneers gave up farming in favor of ranching. Although church leaders implored them to stay, and although they built sturdy stone and brick houses, many (if not most) of the original pioneer families eventually moved on to better prospects elsewhere. Most of Bluff's current residents are descendants of later arrivals.

Beginning in 1963, water backed behind Glen Canyon Dam flooded the channel of the Colorado River below Hole-in-the-Rock. The lowest portion of the trail there is submerged now, although the rise of Lake Powell has made boat access to the hole much easier.

Modern explorers can still visit the fort in Bluff, restored by the Hole-in-the-Rock Foundation. They can also follow the pioneers' route south

Covered wagon at the Hole-in-the-Rock Interpretive Center, Escalante, Utah. *Mormon Pioneer National Heritage Area.*

Educational program at the Hole-in-the-Rock Interpretive Center, Escalante, Utah. *Mormon Pioneer National Heritage Area.*

from Utah Highway 12 to Hole-in-the-Rock itself, although the last five miles are difficult even for four-wheel-drive vehicles. Sections of the hole have fallen in, and the fill the pioneers used to even out the grade is gone. Still, the road's path is clear. Standing at the brink, it's easy to imagine how the wagon drivers must have felt taking the reins while staring into the drop beyond their terrified animals…and then, over the edge!

Special thanks go to Lamont Crabtree, author of *The Incredible Mission: The Hole-in-the-Rock Expedition* (1980), for his photographs of the trail of the San Juan Mission.

LOST TREASURES OF THE MORMON HERITAGE HIGHWAY

BY STEVEN J. CLARK

What could be more exciting than the thought of discovering buried treasure or stumbling across the entrance to a long-lost gold mine? Utah lore is replete with tales of "lost" riches, and the Highway 89 Mormon Heritage Highway corridor is no exception.

My family enjoys such a legend. As a ten-year-old, I was wide-eyed with excitement as my dad and I heard my great-grandfather William (Bill) Clark tell about his father, who supposedly knew where there was gold in Rock Canyon, just east of Provo. Grandpa Bill (that's what my dad called him) said his dad would sneak out of his home in the dead of night and return a day or two later with pockets full of gold. He said that the family would live off the riches until the abundance ran out and another middle-of-the-night trip was needed.

One day, when we visited Great-Granddad's home, which overlooked Provo from atop the Orem Hill, he stood on his rickety porch, pointed at a spot high on the north wall of Rock Canyon and said, "There it is, boys." I could never tell exactly where he was pointing. Nor could I understand why he had never gone up there to get some gold for himself so that he could maybe paint the house…or even buy a new one. But I was thrilled that I knew "almost exactly" where the Clark family secret gold mine was. To this day, it remains a secret—to everyone.

Long before Mormon pioneers settled in Salt Lake Valley, Spanish miners plied the mountains of Utah, searching for gold. According to Spanish government records, they found a fair amount. Prominently mentioned in

Spanish history is the area around Hoyt's Peak near present-day Kamas. When I was just out of high school, my girlfriend's grandfather John W. Young had a cabin on Hoyt's Peak. He had searched the area for Spanish gold for many years. He told me of his discovery of three-foot-tall manmade pyramids, which he claimed were built by the Spanish as markers for their gold explorations. He showed me a cave not far from his cabin whose ceiling had collapsed. We crawled across the top of the slab of the collapsed ceiling until it became too narrow for us to go any farther. Then, with a flashlight, he showed me what looked to be the top of a log wall at the rear of the cave. He said, "That's where the gold is. They refined it and stored it behind that wall. All I've got to do is get some dynamite and blast this rock away."

Shortly thereafter, I left on an LDS mission, and my girlfriend married someone else. I never saw Grandpa Young again and never learned if he realized his dream of excavating the cave. I understand he died in 1983.

At the southern end of the Highway 89 Mormon Heritage Highway, near Kanab, two similar legends of lost treasure live on.

JOHN HUBBELL'S WHITE CLIFFS GOLD

In 1870, seventeen-year-old John Lorenzo Hubbell worked as a sutler's clerk at Fort Wingate, near Gallup, New Mexico. In the course of his work, he befriended an old prospector by the name of George Brankerhoff, who told him a story that set Hubbell on a decades-long search for hidden treasure. Brankerhoff described a cavern filled with white quartz stalactites infused with gold. He said that he found the cavern while prospecting in the White Cliffs of Kane County, Utah, and gave Hubbell specific directions how to get there. The next day, the old man was gone, and although Hubbell tried to track him down, he was never able to find out where Brankerhoff went. But he never forgot the conversation.[15]

Three years later, following Brankerhoff's directions, Hubbell set out to find the cavern. He traveled to Kanab, Utah, and then followed Johnson Creek north and made his way to the White Cliffs. Brankerhoff had told Hubbell that he needed to find a V-shaped cleft pointing downward, but the cleft would appear to be closed by fallen sandstone. According to Brankerhoff, there was a narrow space Hubbell could squeeze through, and once he passed the opening, he would find a cavernous space where the icicle-like quartz stalactites would be found.

White Cliff with cleft, typical of many found in Johnson Canyon, White Cliffs area of Kane County, Utah. *Steven J. Clark.*

Hubble searched for several weeks but was never able to find the V-shaped opening. He broke off his search and traveled sixty-five miles north to Panguitch, Utah, to try to glean more information from local residents.

He took a job as a clerk in a general store but said the locals did not treat him kindly due to his Mexican heritage (on his mother's side). Then he made a critical mistake for a young Roman Catholic man living in a staunchly Mormon community: he took up with a local Mormon girl who also had the eye of the local Mormon bishop. The situation led to a gunfight in which no one was hurt, but shortly thereafter Hubbell was attacked by a dozen local men. Hubbell claimed that he killed two of his attackers but was himself wounded in the fight. He stole a horse and made his way to Lee's Ferry, Arizona, before returning to his home in Parajito, New Mexico. A few years later, in 1878, he founded the first of his chain of highly successful Indian Trading Posts.

But Hubbell still dreamed of finding the White Cliffs gold. He enticed a number of itinerant prospectors to look for the cavern in return for grubstaking them. All were unsuccessful. Then, in 1891, at his trading post at Gallup, New Mexico, Hubbell met Warren Peters, a seasoned sixty-one-year-old prospector who had just sold two silver claims in the San Juan Mountains of southwestern Colorado. Peters was passing through New Mexico on his way to the gold camps of Arizona's Mogollon Mountains.

Seizing on the opportunity to work with a proven, successful prospector, Hubbell told Peters the story of the White Cliffs gold. Taken with the story, Peters let Hubbell persuade him to travel to Hubbell's home in Ganado, Arizona, where Hubbell filled in the details. The two struck a partnership deal, and Hubbell drew Peters a map.

In May 1891, Peters set out for Kane County, Utah, where, using Hubbell's careful directions, Peters found the cavern and the gold-laden quartz stalactites. He knocked down several, claiming that they scattered chunks of gold as they fell, and then filled several pouches with gold and set out for the railhead at Marysville, more than ninety miles to the north. From there, he caught a train to Salt Lake City to sell his gold, only to discover that it had to be shipped to Denver to be refined. He waited more than a month to receive his payment, a substantial one, which finally came in August 1891.

Peters immediately resupplied himself and headed back to relocate the secret cavern, but this time his luck didn't hold. Try as he might, he was unable to find the *V* that marked the location of the tiny cleft. He searched until winter drove him out and then returned to Arizona to tell Hubbell of his adventure.

Stumped by Peters's inability to find the cavern when he'd found it so easily the first time, the pair spent the winter planning for both of them to return to Kane County in the spring. But when spring came, Hubbell had to stay and tend to his business. In his place he sent his friend Henry "Wild Hank" Sharp and two Navajo Indians, Little Chanter and Black Horse. The four left Ganado on April 5, 1892, along with twenty pack mules laden with food and supplies.

When the party reached the White Cliffs, Peters was surprised to find cattle herds grazing in the area. Thinking that to be no problem, the prospectors set up camp at the base of the cliffs near a small spring. The next day, they split into pairs and began their search for the elusive V-shaped notch. Peters and Sharp were the first to return to camp that evening and found six men awaiting them. They saw that their things had been gone through. Asking why the men had taken such liberties, the leader of the bunch said that it was his cattle they'd seen grazing and that there were many cattle thieves in the area. Peters told the man that the land was public domain and that they were prospectors with no interest in cattle. Nonetheless, the cowboy told Peters, in

Hubbell Trading Post at Ganado, Arizona, located twenty miles west of Window Rock, Arizona. *Steven J. Clark.*

no uncertain terms, that he and his party would have to leave. Peters's group elected to abandon their camp at the White Cliffs and move four miles east to Deer Springs Wash.

For several days, they continued searching the White Cliffs but worried continually about the cowboys. One day, when they returned to camp, the Navajos found unidentified tracks that indicated someone had been in their camp. They discussed what to do and decided to search one more day and then leave. In the midst of their discussion, Peters and Sharp spied fifteen riders coming in from the west. The men took up their arms and hid in the sagebrush and boulders.

The riders rode boldly into the camp, the leader shouting that he was the sheriff of Kane County and declaring that Peters and his crew were cattle rustlers. He demanded that they show themselves. Peters shouted back from his hiding place that he didn't believe the man was the sheriff and that the accusation was false. Soon bullets were flying. Having the advantage of cover, Peters and his men were able to force the cowboys away from their camp, but in the process, Peters took a bullet in the leg. With the cowboys temporarily forced away from the camp, Sharp bandaged Peters's wound while the Navajos packed the mules. The prospectors rode throughout the night and did not make camp again until they were well across the Arizona border.[16]

The group tarried for several days to allow Peters's leg to heal and then made its way back to rendezvous with Hubbell. Hubbell and Peters decided that the price of recovering the gold was too high if it chanced someone getting killed. Hubbell never again tried to send prospectors into Utah. Rumors later circulated that someone, presumably the cowboy who ran Peters and his group off, had blown the crevice closed to prevent other prospectors from intruding on the cattleman's range.

The legend of the lost cavern of gold persists in the area today, but the White Cliffs of Kane County are now a part of the Grand Staircase National Monument, making the area off-limits to treasure hunting.

THREE LAKES: MONTEZUMA'S LOST TREASURE

Most travelers driving south to Kanab down Highway 89 are unaware that they have passed within mere yards of what is claimed to be a lost treasure site. The place is called Three Lakes and is located on the west side of the road, about six miles north of the city. The lakes would best be described as ponds rather than bodies of water whose size would elevate them to legitimate "lakes." Travelers see the largest and southernmost of the three right beside the highway. The colorful sandstone cliff that forms the western shore of the third pond has a distinctive rock overhang guarding what looks to be the entrance to a flooded cave. But Brandt Child, owner of the property, claimed that the lake hides a mysterious manmade tunnel that leads to the final repository of Montezuma's lost treasure.

The legend of Montezuma's treasure began nearly five hundred years ago when eleven Spanish ships carrying nearly two thousand people landed on Mexico's eastern shore at what later would become the port city of Veracruz. Included in the passenger list were some six hundred conquistadors, led by Hernán Cortés (Cortez). Hearing stories of gold and silver, Cortés led his conquistadors west into the mountains of Mexico and discovered Tenochtitlan, the capital of the great Aztec civilization, then ruled by the emperor Montezuma. Montezuma mistakenly thought the white-skinned men with shining hair were the fulfillment of the prophecy of Quetzalcoatl, the Aztec sun god, who, legend said, would one day return to claim the Aztec throne.

Hoping to retain his post as emperor and avoid the fulfillment of the prophesy, Montezuma sent Cortés lavish gifts and invited him to go back where he came from. But the gifts included many objects of gold and silver, which was why the Spaniards were there in the first place. They declined Montezuma's invitation and stayed.

On November 18, 1519, Montezuma reluctantly welcomed the Spaniards into the city as gods. He again lavished gold and silver on the visitors and requested that they leave, but the treasure only intensified their greed. Cortés placed Montezuma under house arrest and then set up his headquarters in one of the nearby Aztec temples. From there the Spaniards terrorized the city, ransacking the place and slaughtering many of its inhabitants in their lust for more treasure. Among their discoveries was a hidden treasure vault in Montezuma's palace that, records say, took the Spaniards three days to fully divide between themselves.[17]

On June 30, 1520, the people who remained in the city rose up against not only the Spanish tyranny but also Montezuma himself. They threw the Spaniards out of the palace and stoned Montezuma to death. Then they drove Cortés and his conquistadors out of the city at a horrendous loss of life on both sides. It is said that there were so many corpses in the city's canals that one could walk across them like a bridge. Ever after, the night has been known as *La Noche Triste* (the Sad Night).

Cortés was out of the city, but not out of Mexico. He retreated to Veracruz, where over the next year he rebuilt his core army of conquistadors and assembled an indigenous army of more than five thousand Tlaxcalan (a tribe who were longtime enemies of the Aztecs) soldiers in preparation for a second and final invasion of Tenochtitlan.

Knowing that the city would never stand against the Spaniards' superior arms and their now huge army, the Aztecs gathered what was left of their national treasure hoping to hide it. Theories about the final resting place of Montezuma's treasure abound. Some think it still rests in the layers of mud and silt that are the foundation for the asphalt and concrete of modern-day Mexico City. Others believe the Spaniards gathered it from the canals and put it on an ill-fated ship to Spain that was lost at sea. Still others believe the treasure went south to Costa Rica. But the most persistent stories say that the vast Aztec treasure was gathered by the priests and sent to the far north on the back of slaves, to a land so far away that the priests believed the Spanish would never follow. Legend has it that the priests killed the slaves so that they could never reveal the treasure's hiding place.

Petroglyphs of Fremont Indians in the Fremont Indian State Park and Museum. *Utah State Parks*.

Fast-forward to 1914, when a man by the name of Freddie Crystal walked down Main Street in Kanab with a map in hand that he claimed revealed the hiding place of Montezuma's famous treasure horde. Crystal was an outsider who knew little of the area. Locals told him that the map resembled the location of a collection of white cliffs just northeast of town.[18]

Crystal scoured the area for years, vainly trying to find what he was looking for. Then he stumbled across some Moqui steps carved into the face of a canyon wall that led to carvings in the rock near three sandstone tunnels. Crystal investigated and found that one of the tunnels was blocked off by some sort of manmade stone and mortar.[19]

Crystal enlisted the help of local folks by promising to share the treasure he was sure was about to be unearthed. Soon a sizable contingent of the residents of Kanab had tents pitched at the base of the white cliffs of Cottonwood and Skutumpah Canyons. Although they dug for months, all they found were a few Native American artifacts and some ancient human remains.[20] Town members slowly dwindled away and returned to their homes, but Crystal remained convinced that he was just around the corner

Sandstone caves in Kanab Creek Canyon, located six miles north of Kanab, Utah.
Steven J. Clark.

from discovering Montezuma's treasure. He spent several years plying the canyons around Kanab as he pressed his search in vain.

Fast-forward again to 1989, and enter one Brandt Child, owner of a piece of a property with three small lakes on it that lies along Highway 89. Child advanced the theory that Montezuma's treasure lies hidden below the surface of the largest of the three lakes, located six miles north of Kanab. Child claims that he found an Aztec treasure sign, a circle with a downward pointing arrow, carved in the rock several feet above the water. He says that the location fits with an Aztec technique for hiding treasure called a

Three Lakes, the location of a submerged cave alleged to contain Montezuma's lost treasures. *Steven J. Clark.*

"water trap."[21] As to the legend of Freddie Crystal and the good townsfolk of Kanab in the early twentieth century, Child believes that the caves they explored farther to the east were part of a ploy to obscure the treasure's real hiding place in Kanab Creek Canyon.

Tony Thurber, one of Child's friends, made an exploration dive into the lake and claimed to have discovered what he says is a manmade tunnel under the surface that is four feet wide and seven feet tall and extends a considerable distance west into the cliff face. Thurber added that he made it thirty feet into the tunnel before becoming disoriented, not being able to tell up from down or in from out. He said that there is a strong current in the tunnel and that he feared being swept into an underground river. He made his way out and made another dive, this time with a tether line held by one of his friends on shore. He soon resurfaced, claiming that the tether line was limp rather than taut. The person holding the line said it had been taut throughout the dive.

On June 22, 1989, Thurber returned with three other professional divers, who brought along sonar equipment. The divers said that they got seventy feet into the tunnel and that their equipment showed the tunnel to be one hundred feet long and ending in a room eighty feet in diameter. The sonar equipment allegedly detected the presence of heavy metal at the end of the tunnel.[22]

One of the divers, Russ, said that he had a dream that night in which he swam back into the tunnel, only to find an Aztec warrior who threw a spear at him as he surfaced. And Russ was the first to go down the next morning. Once he got into the tunnel, at some point he started screaming because it felt as if someone was grabbing and choking him. People who pulled him from the water said that he was "white as a sheet." Another diver went down and experienced the same sensation. They tried the dive again two weeks later, but the dive ended the same way, so they never returned to the lake.

Child determined that the only way to get to the bottom of the mystery was to drain the lake and explore the tunnel for himself. But intervention by the U.S. Fish and Wildlife Service thwarted his plan. It seems that the three ponds are home to an endangered species of snail, the Kanab amber snail, found nowhere else in the world. Fish and Wildlife has fenced off the lakes and prohibited any activity that it deems threatening to the tiny mollusk.

In December 1991, someone mysteriously placed eleven geese in the pond. Fish and Wildlife personnel rounded up the geese and forced them to vomit, saying that it was an obvious attempt to kill the snails, although they couldn't name any suspects. The fine for killing one of the endangered little fellows is $50,000 per snail.[23]

Plans to drill through the rock at the back of the tunnel have been made, but to date, the reports are that the drills break or otherwise are mysteriously stopped just short of the chamber.

So, does Montezuma's long-lost treasure exist just a few yards away from where thousands of travelers whisk along Highway 89, just a few miles from downtown Kanab? Who knows, but if we ever hear a news story of some hapless traveler being impaled on an Aztec spear when he decided to hop the fence and take a cool, refreshing dip in lake number three, then we'll know that Montezuma's ghostly warriors are still at work protecting the boss's treasure.

Chapter 3

CLARION:
A Back-to-the-Soil Movement

By Eileen Hallet Stone

Picture this: three miles southwest of Gunnison in Sanpete County, there was located one of the largest Jewish agrarian colonies west of the Appalachian Mountains. It took root in 1911 and failed, but it was not for lack of trying. It was marginal land—an alluvial fan at the foot of mountains, semi-arid, desolate, steep, rock-studded and sparse with rolling tumbleweed and sagebrush. Yet for a brief time it was a settlement of hope and promise called Clarion, composed of immigrant families instilled with the belief that "agriculture will make laborers instead of paupers [and] bread producers instead of bread beggars."[24]

Between 1880 and 1920, 2 million eastern European Jews immigrated to America's urban cities. Poor and overwhelmed by teeming streets, slums, "sweatshop slavery," congested tenements, crime, discrimination and economic oppression, some yearned for greener pastures. They listened intently as activists praised the virtues of farming and the back-to-the-soil movement that was sweeping the country.

Russian emigrant and activist Benjamin Brown was the backbone of Clarion Colony's back-to-the-soil experience.[25] Agitating for a nonreligious Jewish cooperative farming community, he reasoned that such colonies would free Jews from urban ghettos and provide them opportunities to become self-reliant and prosper.

"When living in the *shtetls* of Europe, Jews were forbidden to own land, and very few of them were farmers," explained Robert Goldberg, author of *Back to the Soil.* "Clarion would be their trumpet call; their shofar calling them out of the city and back to the land."[26]

Speaking in Yiddish to groups in Philadelphia, New York and Baltimore under the umbrella of the newly formed Jewish Agricultural and Colonial Association, Brown paralleled the importance of working together as farmers with improving the economic future for America Jews, combating anti-Semitism and creating goodwill among Christian neighbors. His speeches and compelling charm appealed to working people of all kinds, from accountants, peddlers and clerks to plumbers, stonemasons and electricians, as well as to those representing different branches of Judaism and political affiliations, including religious Orthodox, socialists, Zionists, communists, nationalists, anarchists and atheists.

Pragmatically, the twenty-four-year-old proposed that religion would remain a private matter, politics a personal affair and Judaism celebrated for its history and tradition rather than ritual observance. Idealistically, he promoted an agrarian settlement composed of privately owned homes with collective support for cultivating fields, purchasing large farm equipment and selling the colony's goods and produce.

"[Brown sought] 150 to 200 young married men with approximately three hundred dollars each whose savings would generate an operating capital between forty-five thousand and sixty thousand dollars for the purchase of land, equipment, livestock and building materials," Goldberg explained. Fascinated by Brown's vision, many such men enthusiastically joined and supported the association and, in preparation, attended classes at state agricultural colleges or the National Farm School founded by Rabbi Joseph Krauskopf in Philadelphia.

The association quickly advertised for land in major western newspapers and queried state agricultural agencies. In early 1911, Brown and association partner Isaac Herbst, a socialist and civil engineer, headed west seeking enough land for a large settlement with "virgin soil," water sources and accessibility to markets. Disappointed with costly land prices in New Mexico and Colorado, they were advised to go to Utah and took heart. The state was actively seeking future settlers. When agents from the Utah State Board of Land Commissioners showed what was purported to be choice, arable land in south-central Utah, Brown and Herbst were elated. About five miles long, three miles wide and a half mile from the Sevier River, the six-thousand-acre parcel stretched out below the state-promised Piute Canal, the construction costs of which would be alleviated by the land sale.

The association bought the property and water rights at a public land auction for nearly $69,000—10 percent down, ten-year balance due. Clarion's proximity to Gunnison's railroad line was a plus, as the Denver

Portrait of the David Bernstein family before leaving New York to join the Clarion Colony: Michael (second from left), Louis (second from right) and Harry (right). *Robert Goldberg*

and Rio Grande Railroad offered direct transportation to Salt Lake City and beyond. Once settled, colonists would use the rails to transport their produce throughout the west and back east. Traveling to Gunnison's depot by buckboard, they welcomed newcomers, who, dressed in city clothes and carrying umbrellas, were bewildered by the enormity of open space.

Colonist David Bernstein's son Harry never forgot the experience. "When it was decided that our family was going [to Clarion] the effect upon [us] had an aura of a dreamlike sense of adventure and excitement, going to some wonderful faraway place, full of hope and promise," he wrote. "By the time we left in 1912 our family had grown to six children, the oldest being nine. The trip, which took three days, was memorable. Leaving our drab home, boarding one of the most luxurious trains of those days, and watching the fascinating scenery as we travelled exceeded anything we could have imagined."[27]

Another colonist, Moshe Malamed, was astonished at the sight of former city dwellers and friends greeting him at the station. "All the men were so sunburned, it was hard to recognize them," he wrote. "I [saw] glowing, dark eyes beneath a forehead covered with long, uncut hair. We waved at each other warmly, and still I didn't know whose hand I was pressing. 'Don't you recognize me?' he laughed. I am stunned. We embrace."[28]

IN 1911, TWELVE ÉMIGRÉS led by Brown entered Sanpete County anxious to clear land, plow, plant, harvest and cultivate a new life, eventually, for more than two hundred Jews. Two men had farming experience. The others were chosen for leadership qualities and knowledge of animals, construction and fieldwork. They surveyed the land to subdivide into forty-acre homesteads for the first fifty families and laid plans for a main road. They constructed a communal farm; pitched four large tents for living, dining and sleeping; hauled in water from Gunnison; and purchased a modern tractor for tilling.

According to the September 15, 1911 *Gunnison Gazette*, "The advance guard is quite busy, having in operation a large gasoline power plow which is made to do a capacity of twenty acres a day. The plow was adjusted in Gunnison by representatives of the firm which made the sale, and being the first to be brought into this section it attracted quite a big crowd of onlookers."

Planning Clarion's future: Benjamin Brown (second from right) and Isaac Herbst (right). *Robert Goldberg.*

Eager to clear the land of rocks, the new farmers quickly discovered that the soil considered "choice" was anything but—in most areas, the gravelly and sandy loam was underlain by an impervious layer of clay-like subsoil. Large parcels of hilly land sloped "steeply," and others were too close to ravines to be developed into productive fields. Nevertheless, Governor William Spry sent advisors from Utah State Agricultural College to instruct the colonists on dry farming irrigation techniques and crop selection. Mormon neighbors in Gunnison, whose fields teemed with alfalfa, oats and wheat, also lent a helping hand.

Buoyed by the camaraderie, the colonists greeted each sunrise with "song and labor" and every sunset with "restfulness and spiritual happiness." Isaac Friedlander, one of the original twelve settlers, described the boundless enthusiasm shared by the early colonists: "[Today] one man at the supper table tells that for the first time he plowed a large area with the help of an eight-horse team, and Joseph Furman, called the 'Fifteener' because

he wears a size 15 shoe, often declares, 'Let us make a good go of it here, and you'll see the whole Jewish people returning to the land.'"[29] By fall, the men had cleared 1,500 acres for spring planting and dug irrigation ditches, ecstatically waiting for the first sign of greening.

Enthralled by his new surroundings, Friedlander extolled the sights and colors of autumn: meadow grasses that "glisten golden in the sunshine so radiant," mountain walls tinged in "hued rose and yellow," late afternoons of "blueness" and "gigantic" trees that that made them "moths by comparison, [but] greater than our ordinary selves because we had had this transcendental experience."

During winter, the colonists encountered setbacks. Heavy

With hope for a good harvest. *Robert Goldberg.*

A new life in farming for Abe Sendrow. *Eileen Hallet Stone.*

snowfall often cut off their connection with Gunnison, and they couldn't shop for staples or pick up their longed-for mail with family news from home. Unaware of Sanpete County's short growing season, they were also misinformed about its weather and, thinking it was mostly temperate, left behind their warm winter clothing.

They then faced an economic crisis. The association's resources—largely spent on livestock, material, tools, machinery and working wages (colonists were paid fifteen dollars per week)—were running out. Goods bought on credit were now due, and the state's first installment for the land was called in. Rushing back east to solicit more funds and recruit new association members—raising fees to help offset actual costs—Brown never wavered in his enthusiasm and returned to Clarion with nearly $6,000. When the state deferred payment for another year, the funds were redirected into the colony's coffers, and a relieved community was given the financial go-ahead for spring.

Waiting out the winter amid the mournful howling of the coyotes, the colonists read agricultural literature, wrote letters home, kept journals, debated God's existence and questioned the fate of capitalism while singing, mending harnesses and honing their tools. In the February thaw, they cleared more land of stones, plowed and planted oats, corn, alfalfa and wheat. On the steeper slopes, they crosshatched marks deeply into the earth, creating channels to redirect water and prevent soil erosion. As more families arrived, the new men took to the fields, while others turned their attention to building homes. By late spring, sprouts appeared in the fields with the promise of a good crop.

If cities are schools of hard knocks, farms are lessons in hard rocks. Strong winds, dust storms, heat, dry wells, lack of water and swarms of

Russian attire in American fields. *Eileen Hallet Stone.*

mosquitoes plagued the farmers. The prized tractor was difficult to maintain and expensive. No one in the colony knew how to repair the equipment, and hired mechanics needed to trek to Clarion to finesse it into working.

Managing water was an unending challenge and frustration. To help store water for livestock, Isaac Herbst oversaw the construction of a concrete cistern. Digging a ditch from the canal, workers unearthed a portion of a hill to support three abutting eight-foot-high cistern walls. They poured cement into building forms, added a fourth restraining wall, attached a faucet and filtration system and covered the top. After the cement cured, they slowly filled the cistern with water and celebrated. Days later, the colonists were jarred awake by a loud rumble. Built with inferior cement and lacking reinforcing rods, an unsupported wall was blown to the ground and shattered, the water saturating the earth.

When the Piute Canal was finally brought closer to the colony and laterals extended into the fields, the water, expected before the irrigation season, was late in coming. It flowed for a week, covered one-third of the fields and then disappeared. Whether the canal could not contain the volume of water needed, had not sufficiently settled, was poorly constructed or was weakened by burrowing animals and leached in transit, repairs left the colony without a drop of water for thirty-three days.

Fearful of losing more crops, Brown telegraphed the Board of Land Commissioners and the Sevier Valley Canal Company for help. Admittedly, the new farmers were "unskilled" in irrigation techniques, but two days of "enough" water to irrigate the entire 1,500 acres was simply not enough, and stream levels fluctuated. What did grow was barely enough to pay for the seeds. "The deficit naturally reacted adversely on the spirit of all of us," Brown wrote.

Accusations laced with "I told you so" raged. Some colonists, losing confidence in Brown, sent letters of complaint to the association, which tightened its financial support. The state insisted on being paid its first installment. The firm that sold the marvelous but unpredictable gas-powered tractor reneged on its original "after cultivation" payment agreement.

Brown immediately went to Salt Lake City for support. Early on, the city's philanthropic Jewish leaders—such as railroad magnate Simon Bamberger, elected Utah's first Democrat and only Jewish governor in 1917; Samuel Newhouse, who constructed the city's first skyscrapers; and the Auerbach brothers, renowned for building one of the first department stores in the West—endorsed Clarion's back-to-the-soil concept. Working with attorney Daniel Alexander, they created the Utah Colonization Fund, a "help-organization" that became a holding company for Clarion securities. Now, Brown wrote, he was "left to peddle with this pack of bonds."

Salt Lake's Jewry bought bonds for $5,000. Bamberger donated $2,000 worth of lumber to build houses. Again, Brown's unflagging resolve earned more funding, and with a loan from the Gunnison bank and another state reprieve, Clarion looked toward another season with a caveat: the colony had voted to divide the land into individual farms, each with four acres and a house.

"When we first arrived, the home we were to live in was not yet completed so we were all crowded together, two adults and six children, in our temporary shelter, a crudely built shack of two small rooms." Harry wrote. "Our furniture hadn't arrived. We slept on the floor, using blankets and pillows my father had purchased. But with few exceptions there was a cooperative spirit among the colonists. They gave their time and labor, and pooled their skills and experience to aid one another whenever necessary."

Joseph Furman, a carpenter by trade, helped the elder Bernstein and other colonists build four-room wood-frame houses with gabled roofs and brick chimneys. "Mr. Furman was my father's kinsman," second son Michael recalled. "He and Pa built houses on a concrete foundation at intervals along the main road. We regarded them as the epitome of luxury. I continued to

A family home in Clarion. *Robert Goldberg.*

sleep on the top of the family trunk. The girls slept in the living room. Harry and Louis slept in one bedroom, and Pa and Ma slept in the other."[30]

These newer homes had central heating. "That is, they had a wood burning stove in the kitchen," Michael explained. "To get water, Pa would take a barrel, or hogshead, put it on the wagon, drive down to the Sevier River and fill it with river water. He'd put it outside the kitchen door and cover it with a wooden cover. In winter, mother would crack the ice in the barrel, heat water on the stove, and pour it into a washbasin for us to successively climb in to bathe...It was a Friday night ritual."

The Bernstein family living on the farm. *Robert Goldberg.*

Before the colony built its school in 1913, the children traveled several miles to attend school in nearby Centerfield. David Bernstein adapted a hackney wagon with a small stove in the center to keep them warm during the hour-long winter runs. They were fond of their principal, athletic coach and teacher Charles Embley Jr., and were delighted when his father, Embley Sr., later taught at their school in Clarion.

"Like the other homes in Clarion, the school was a lumber structure on a concrete foundation divided into two classrooms with unplastered walls and a stove for heating," Harry remembered. "Each room had about twelve desks, a blackboard and textbooks. Mr. Embley was a kindly man. He divided his time between the two classrooms—the oldest child then was about ten—and we were eager to learn so there were few problems among us."

For many colonists, though, selecting the school's curriculum was a bitter lesson. "What began in harmony and cooperation degenerated into bitter feuding when the program of Jewish education was considered," Goldberg explained. "Dissension and debate can only be understood in the context of the ideological diversity that pervaded the Jewish immigrant world."

Nationalists emphasized Jewish identity taught by a teacher who had an understanding of the Yiddish language, tradition and text. Radicals required students to understand the basics of socialism. Hebrew rites and services were essentials for the more religious Jews. Others were satisfied with the school board's choice of the Mormon teacher from Centerfield. Compromises were eventually made, but it left a fair amount of grumbling and sour taste in the mouths of some.

The school building was also used for holding meetings, religious services, holidays, celebrations and fairs. "But ideological cracks had grown wider and more exposed," Goldberg wrote, "seriously weakening Clarion's base." Although 5 families left the colony, the 150 families who remained endeavored to make Clarion their home. Setting aside internal differences, spirits once again were raised.

It was difficult work. The men labored. The women were busy. Sarah Bernstein, who brought her Sabbath candlestick holders, made the family's butter and cheese and baked challah on Fridays. Like other Clarion women, she also kept a tidy home, tended an income-producing garden, took care of the farm animals, raised chickens, milked cows, hauled water, cooked, washed and mended clothes, worked in the fields if necessary and, when pregnant, made the round-trip journey to see the doctor or midwife in Gunnison.

"My mother was scrupulously clean and without being fanatical was very religious which increased her work in many ways," Harry wrote. "With three sets of dishes, for milk foods, meat foods, and Passover, she took on the task of keeping track of, storing, and cleaning each separately, as required by the rituals…There was no refrigeration so we made use of the daily supply from our own cow with the excess allowed to turn sour. Meat, from locally slaughtered chickens or lambs, was cooked and consumed within a day or two, and when purchased from town was kept from spoiling with ice wrapped in burlap given by the butcher."

Homegrown vegetables were eaten fresh, canned or pickled. Michael remembered eating garden cucumbers sliced in a bowl of sour cream—"the most mouth-watering dish I can think of"—and walking into the fields to "pull up a fresh turnip, wipe off the soil with our hands and eat it raw with relish." He also recalled Mormon neighbors inviting the children to pick plums in their overbearing orchards: "We ate plum jelly, plum jam, and canned plums to our heart's delight and sometimes to satiety."

Both boys remembered Clarion as an adventure from day to night. After completing school lessons and farm chores, life was an "excitement that more than made up for any of the physical deprivations that such a life leads to." They went on hayrides; rode horseback; floated in the deep, saline water–filled "salt mine" pit; hiked mountain trails; explored the Sevier River; decorated for community-held festivities; and grew country-strong, determined, lean and healthy. "I suppose it would have shocked people in the city to think we went to sleep listening to the howling of the coyotes at night and might on occasion look out the window and see a pack of coyotes roaming near the hen house," Harry wrote. "Pa kept a rifle in the house. But usually when the coyotes were around, we were out of ammunition. When we had plenty, they didn't show up."

In summer 1913, 2,400 acres of land were greening. Overnight the sky darkened, and rain clouds appeared. Anticipation turned to dread. Heavy rains pummeled Clarion. Violent runoff from the Valley Mountains and water-engorged canals drowned the sprouting fields. "A heroic storm, the roaring of the mountain winds, and torrents racing from the hills carrying rocks intermingling with the unceasing thunder and lightning terrified us." Friedlander wrote.

After a second and third storm struck the fields, the demoralized colony became more divided. Hopes unraveled in anger and despair. Then, heartbreakingly, one of the most experienced farmers, twenty-nine-year-old Aaron Binder, died. Homeward bound after harvesting timber in the mountains at seven thousand feet, his full wagon overturned and he was crushed. Eulogizing Binder, Friedlander wrote that he was "a son of the people, a humble hardworking Jew, with a great Jewish soul, he died a martyr, in the cause of raising our level and not permitting shame on the Jewish name."

Buried in Clarion's small cemetery, Binder was soon joined by his infant son, who died of meningitis. The following year, devoted colonist and family man David Bernstein also died tragically, of gangrene.

Struggling to farm with dwindling funds and water shortages, Goldberg wrote, "The colonists had compounded their water problems with incompetence. They planted wheat developed for dry farming, which

Historic Liberal Hall. *Wasatch Academy.*

school he offered to start. Historian Theodore Martin contended that McMillan "came to Mt. Pleasant, representing no organized institution, but as an unemployed minister. The opinion of those intimately familiar with the Presbyterian work in the inter-mountain area was against his coming to Mt. Pleasant." McMillan defied those cautions. Whether McMillan came on formal business or not, he did not deny who he was or what he did. He was a preacher and a teacher, the likes of which Mount Pleasant had never seen before.

Soon after arriving in Mount Pleasant, he secured Liberal Hall (for a price of $1,000), but he could not secure carpenters to furnish the building. He also failed to find another church willing to loan him any furniture. He secured two hundred feet of lumber and borrowed the tools necessary to build his own desks. By his own hand he readied his school for opening, and on April 19, 1875—six weeks after arriving in Mount Pleasant—the school now known as Wasatch Academy was born.[37] However, while today the school's anniversary is marked by celebration and camaraderie between faculty, students and alumni, in 1875 McMillan's school opening was marked by tension and conflict with the Mormon leadership.

When Dr. Henry Kendall, the first Presbyterian to preach in Utah, asked Brigham Young if it would be safe to send Presbyterian missions to Utah, Young replied, "Should such a missionary find anyone who wanted to hear him he supposed that he would not be molested."[38] In light of what would later unfold, Young's promise seemed to be little more than an empty pleasantry—a formality between fellow clergymen. Young told Kendall what he wanted to hear, but as McMillan would later learn, Young's practice would deviate from what he promised.

The Presbyterian and Mormon attitudes came to loggerheads in Mount Pleasant. Historian Linda Simons's description of Utah sets the stage for the conflict between McMillan and the Mormons:

> It had been nearly twenty-eight years since the first Mormon settlers had arrived in Utah Territory. For all practical purposes Utah was a social, if not a political, theocracy populated by a refugee people whose memories of persecution and death were yet vivid. They had chosen the desolation of this uninhabited area specifically for that reason and intended not to be molested again. However, with the advent of the Golden Spike, mineral discoveries, and the presence of federal troops and officials, the immigration of Gentiles in significant numbers was imminent; cultural friction was inevitable.[39]

Simons understated the intensity of the situation when she described it as "cultural friction." On one hand, McMillan saw the Sanpete Valley as an errant community devoid of adequate education. Welcomed by apostate Mormons, he saw his work as noble, with the added bonus of any new church members. On the other hand, Mormon leadership saw the introduction of any outside presence—especially a Presbyterian minister and a Presbyterian school—as a direct threat to their way of life.

Young denounced McMillan, his school and all that he stood for. In an oft-repeated quote, Young declared McMillan an enemy of Zion, "an imp of perdition, a minion of Satan, a damn Presbyterian devil." He added, "You know very well how to do it. What would you do if a wolf should jump into your corral and proceed to destroy your sheep? Why you would shoot them at sight. Souls are more precious than sheep and it becomes you to be correspondingly diligent in disposing of this intruder."[40]

It is probable that Young was only speaking metaphorically and did not expect his followers to shoot McMillan like a wolf in a sheep corral. Nevertheless, to Young, McMillan had declared war on the Mormon Church. At stake were the souls of the apostates and the sustainability of the Mormon zeitgeist.

Young traveled with his apostles to Mount Pleasant, speaking out for two days against McMillan and all who followed him while simultaneously trying to return all the apostate Mormons to his religion. The Liberals notwithstanding, the majority of Mount Pleasant welcomed Young and his message. Loyal Mormons "erected triumphal floral arches to welcome Brigham, and had hailed him as 'King Brigham' on his arrival." To them, Young's warning came easily: "Keep your children away from that school. If God wants them to know grammar and arithmetic he can inspire them with that knowledge as well as with spiritual truth."[41] In an agrarian community, Young argued, formalized education begat a generation that would not work. In the eyes of Brigham Young, the Sanpete Valley needed more farmers. What he felt they did *not* need was Duncan McMillan.

Rejecting the influence of outside educators and preachers had been a theme that Young often emphasized. Speaking at the September 14, 1874 annual conference, Young said, "Educate a lad and he will want to become a Governor, a judge, and treasurer; you can get no useful work out of him. Free schools make lawyers, doctors, devils of our boys, and quite unfit them for any future usefulness."[42] His message would later be applied to McMillan and especially the apostasy. These ex-Mormons "had banded themselves together to resist the oppression of the priesthood. They had gone into infidelity, which is the usual rebound from Mormonism, and had erected a hall for dancing and social purposes."[43] Worse than dancing, McMillan now added non-Mormon education to the list of apostate offenses. More than moving away from the Mormon Church, now it included a move toward an outsider.

Young's efforts to stop McMillan seemed to work in the short term when the school closed that summer. However, Young's actions backfired, as people from "Mount Pleasant and other communities begged [McMillan] to start schools in their home towns."[44] Young underestimated the power of the growing apostasy and the thirst for education.

McMillan expected resistance from the Mormon leadership to his establishment of the school in Mount Pleasant. To some extent, he expected the personal attacks that followed as well. Verbal harassment and stone throwing seemed to pale in comparison to the more virulent accusations made by Young. He accused McMillan of sodomy and subsisting on beef stolen from good Mormons. Young went as far as to describe McMillan as a "vile, godless man, worse than an infidel, teaching sedition, infidelity—and free love." These slanderous accusations may not have had much traction or caused McMillan to lose sleep. On the other hand, though, threats on McMillan's life brought the conflict to a different level. Young's analogy of a wolf in a sheep's corral led one of Young's zealous followers to boast that "bullets were moulded and ready for use at the first opportunity."[45] The threats on his life kept McMillan alert but not scared.

The boast of bullets proved to be more than apocryphal when McMillan awoke to see an armed assailant outside his window. Only after brandishing his own weapon (a swamp angel, a revolver common to the West at this time) did the would-be assassin back down.[46] Surprised but not unprepared, McMillan would not be routed so easily. McMillan adopted the habit—for his own safety—of sleeping and preaching with a revolver close by. Historian Theodore D. Martin added:

> McMillan had been warned that should he come to his own preaching service, his life would be in danger. Then he did arrive—and he found a crowded house awaiting him—he was cautioned not to continue with the service. In response he invited the Mayor and the Bishop to sit with him on the platform. His invitation was declined. He took his place behind the pulpit laid his revolver upon the open Bible where every eye could see it. "sang a hymn alone, read the scriptures, poured out his soul in prayer

and afterwards preached such a loving gospel that enmity for the time was disarmed."[47]

McMillan prided himself on being able to convince his crowds with the power of his words, but should his words fail, he also considered himself a quick draw. He boasted that he could best any man in the valley in a duel. He conceded that he could easily be outnumbered in a crowd, but he maintained that he would not be the first man to fall.

Preaching with a Bible and a revolver on the pulpit, McMillan remained committed to his mission, his school and his faith, all in the face of Mormon opposition both in the Sanpete Valley and from the apostles up north. In a letter to his mother, McMillan confirmed his commitment but also his fear for his safety. "Now unless the 'Saints' decorate my person with plumage and 'something to make it stick' and bear me in the royal manner beyond the municipal boundaries I shall stay with them awhile." Even Mormons conceded that Young harshly called for an end to McMillan's school and that he encouraged nonattendance (though none admitted to a tar-and-feathering plan). However, regardless of the exact words Young used, his intent was clear. He wanted the enrollment to cease and the school to close. In this regard, Young's words failed in their desired effect, as enrollment quickly soared to 150 students.[48]

The Mormon Church denied harassing McMillan and that Brigham Young and his band of apostles spoke ill of him in Mount Pleasant. Officially, the Mormon Church dismissed the intimidation allegations as lies; however, this contention is countered by outside evidence supporting McMillan's struggles. The Salt Lake City *Daily Tribune* argued that leaders like McMillan were the future of the Utah territory and that myopic Mormon pressures were counterintuitive. "The future of this Territory rests with the character of the young people who in a few years will be active members of society, conducting its affairs, moulding public opinion, and giving birth to and shaping the destiny of the coming generation." The article went on to argue that "the delusion of Mormonism rarely survives the second generation. The sons and daughters of devout Saints grow up with a disgust for the divine ordinance which has branded a stain upon their brows and wrecked the happiness of many thousand homes." The *Daily Tribune* deemed McMillan a harbinger of the future and implored the Mormon Church to heed and give way.[49] McMillan exposed and exploited fissures in the bedrock of Mormondom, and the apostate Utahans were thankful for his efforts.

The *Daily Tribune* contended that McMillan offered superior education, adding that the Mormon Church, with its leadership at the time, stood in the way by instructing its faithful to send "their children to the inferior and unattractive Mormon schools." In their words, McMillan, the "zealous instructor," gathered "the young folks almost without effort." McMillan's presence brought the debate of "church rule or no-church rule" to the forefront, as many locals embraced his teaching and his presence and opposed the Mormon Church's obstruction tactics.[50]

The reporting of the *Daily Tribune*, the more secular and gentile-friendly of Utah's mass dailies, contrasted starkly with the *Deseret News*, the Mormon standard. *Deseret News* editor Charles W. Penrose recounted a different story. In a September 17, 1881 editorial, he characterized the story of McMillan's persecution as "a falsehood from beginning to end" and argued that, in fact, the Mormon community embraced McMillan. Penrose dismissed the pistol story as "a Presbyterian plagiarism of a Methodist fiction." He demonized McMillan for not speaking out more strongly against the slander and libel against Mormons, for not denouncing what Penrose believed to be false claims.[51] Penrose argued that McMillan promised to speak out against alleged animus from Sanpete County locals but that McMillan never did so.

Time gradually eroded the tenacity of Young's position. The longer Wasatch Academy continued to exist, the more established and permanent in the community the school became. A steady stream of apostate Mormons and local community members was eventually joined by other national and international support. Students came from near and far to attend Wasatch Academy, and as a result, Wasatch Academy became a fixture in Mount Pleasant. Within five years, by 1880, it became clear that Wasatch Academy would stand the test of time and the test of Brigham Young.

On March 31, 1880, Reverend R.G. McNiece, pastor of the Presbyterian Church of Salt Lake City, gave encouraging statistics on the success of mission schools in the state. Speaking about Sanpete County (an allusion to McMillan's efforts), McNiece declared, "San Pete [*sic*] has been leavened and the whole mass is set a-moving with the revivifying agency introduced."[52] Nine months later, on December 12, 1880, McMillan left Wasatch Academy and Mount Pleasant. He would return as a visitor and as a patriarch, but he went on to do other things. He started forty other schools and rose to a prominent position in the Presbyterian Church. McMillan died on June 27, 1939, at the age of

Duncan McMillan. *Wasatch Academy.*

ninety-three. Living at the time in New York City, the veteran, preacher and educator touched many lives in his long life.[53]

McMillan left the school, but he also left a legacy. To the patrons, teachers and students of the school, he is a legend. Wasatch Academy is the only one of McMillan's schools still in operation. His stories and accolades are told like sagas. However, McMillan's legacy is larger than Wasatch Academy pride or the annual "Founders Day" celebration of his efforts. McMillan reunited an isolated community with the world. Nearly

Liberal Hall, Wasatch Academy. *Wasatch Academy.*

thirty years after Mormon settlers landed in the Sanpete Valley, a gentile outsider would lift the Zion curtain. There was nothing wrong with those who embraced Young and the Mormon faith in Mount Pleasant, but for those who were dissatisfied, McMillan offered a viable alternative.

Chapter 5

"NAMES MEAN NOTHING": HIRAM BEBEE AKA THE SUNDANCE KID

BY JACK C. BILLINGS

Some residents of Sanpete County, Utah, have quasi-adopted Hiram Bebee, believing him to be the escaped Harry Longabaugh (aka the Sundance Kid). It is a curious sort of adoption because Hiram Bebee shot Mount Pleasant town marshal Alonzo T. Larsen on October 15, 1945. Then he was vilified as a murderer, nicknamed the "Sanpete Slayer." Over the decades, the sting of the marshal's untimely death has faded away, and now some usefulness has grown in its place.

So, was he or wasn't he the Sundance Kid? To answer that, I am going to take a clue from former secretary of state Hillary Clinton's testimony: "What does it matter at this time?" You are not going to hear either the real Kid or this "wannabe," as some have called him, speak at some ribbon-cutting or graduation exercise. Come to Sanpete County to see where a real-life old-time cowboy and gunslinger did his last shooting. This man's last days are deserving of an airing in their own right.

My mother, Delome Sorensen Billings, was the first in our family to meet Hiram Bebee. According to her recollection, it was about eleven years before the incident with Marshal Larsen. That would have made it about 1934. Also in the picture were my maternal grandparents, Mr. and Mrs. Alfred Sorensen, and my father, William E. Billings. Both my mother and grandfather spoke to the Utah Board of Pardons on Bebee's behalf, trying to get his sentence of execution commuted to life in prison at hard labor. I inherited Mother's archive of papers concerning her friend. I also inherited her belief in this revered teacher.

So what do we know for sure about old Hiram Bebee? He was old and small of stature. He had a full head of hair that, along with a full beard and moustache, reached to about mid-chest level. Most Utah residents considered him to be strange on many fronts. On the stand, when asked what kind of life he had led, he said, "[S]ort of drifting."[54] He claimed to have worked in Montana, Wyoming, Arizona and New Mexico. A brief reference was made to Arkansas, so Texas should probably be added to the list also.

He led the Utah Seventh Judicial District Court on a bit of a chase. The court never did get a firm date of birth or place of birth out of him on the stand, nor did he give them his name; he had been sworn in by the name Hiram Beebe, but he also testified to having used other names, not ever stating which one he started out life with. When taken into custody in 1945, he was, of course, fingerprinted. Those prints were sent away to the Federal Bureau of Investigation (FBI) in the hopes of there being a match somewhere in the system. The report came back that this man had done time in California's San Quentin prison. From that report was an estimated age in 1919 of forty-five. So, in Utah at the time of his arrest he would have been seventy-one. Please do keep in mind that this is all extrapolation; it is not at all clear in the Utah trial transcript whether one of the names he had testified to using (George Hanlon) was the one on the San Quentin record. Furthermore, we have no way of knowing if that information was accurate; he may have danced around back in 1919 the same as he did in 1945–48. Such indefiniteness was surely like a goad to both Utah and federal authorities.

The "Sundance Kid" allegation just sort of popped up. No one is on record as claiming to have heard the old man say he was the Sundance Kid. He was being watched closely in prison, with the guards reporting back the rumors heard from the inmates. On the outside, his wife, Glame, and the live-in friend O'Bannion were followed. The allegation/legend was on the back burner just simmering, with folks occasionally giving it a taste as news items about the prison cropped up. To finish the metaphor, one might say the Newman/Redford movie is what got the interest in Butch Cassidy and the Sundance Kid on the public's menu as a historical dining experience.

Anyone who researches the matter naturally forms an opinion. My opinion is this: The prosecution forces in the Seventh Judicial District in Utah were very hot to get more data on Hiram Bebee. Why? They did not need to learn who shot the marshal; multiple people saw Hiram Bebee do the shooting. It was perfectly possible to convict him and execute him with only this name he was using at the time of the shooting. I believe the FBI (and, further back, the Pinkertons) were the ones trying to fill out or complete their

Hiram Bebee. *Alvin Gittins.*

dossiers. It is a black eye for law enforcement to have cases remain open for many years, but many cases do remain open. Worse yet is for suspects to be out running around committing more crimes. Having the public believe that the Sundance Kid had been caught was to law enforcement's advantage. The possibility of a wrongful conviction back in the California record cannot be ruled out, regardless of whether the agencies had a good handle on him. Only DNA analysis can definitively lay the matter to rest.

Frank O'Bannion, July 1954. *Author's collection.*

The man who called himself Hiram Bebee was real, no mistake about that. And his case was a real shooting, although it was not a "shootout" in the classic Hollywood sense of two men facing each other with both hoping to be the fastest. Reading the transcript with a benefit of the doubt going to the defendant, the picture is that Marshal Alonzo T. Larsen got involved with this little old man and lost his cool. He was on the losing side in the earlier verbal exchange, and he wasn't going to have any more of it. It all went downhill from there.

Hiram's first trial was held at Manti in 1946. It was declared a mistrial by the Utah Supreme Court by reason that two prejudicial errors had been made.[55] There was a change of venue made for the second trial at Price, Utah, in June 1947. His testimony in Price was a jewel of almost reckless frankness interspersed with mind-numbing tedium. Judge F.W. Keller presided at Price; the attorneys remained the same as in Manti. Duane Frandsen was the prosecuting attorney, assisted by John McAllister, county attorney for Sanpete County, and Lewis Larsen. Appointed by the state to represent Hiram as his defense counsel was E. Leroy Shields.

THE ALTERCATION

A brief synopsis of the incident is in order. The Bebee group had driven down from Provo, Utah, where they had spent the weekend shopping. The group consisted of Hiram Bebee; his wife, Glame; and Paul Millett, a friend whose pickup truck they were using for this trip. They had come into Mount Pleasant just a little before sundown and had stopped to pick up some bottled beer to take on home to Spring City to another friend, Frank O'Bannion, who had remained behind.

Mrs. Bebee had a cup of coffee and then later on went to a drugstore to purchase a magazine. The two men went into the Kolstrum Beer Parlor to get the beer. Millett handled the purchase of the bottled beer. Hiram had ordered a glass of beer and strode to the back of the tavern. He stopped at a table to speak to a woman he thought he recognized. She became the third defense witness, Mrs. Kate Schofield. Mrs. Schofield was sitting at the table with Pearley Johnson and another man. While Hiram was speaking to her, Johnson reached out and pulled Hiram's hair/beard "to see if it was real." It was a forward, inappropriate thing to do and technically constituted battery. Testimonies differed about Bebee's reaction, but the incident was set aside.

Hiram returned to the bar to set down his glass (only half consumed), preparing to leave. At this point, Alonzo T. Larsen stopped him by putting a hand on his shoulder. A verbal exchange took place. The testimonies later differed, but the gist of the conversation was that Larsen demanded Hiram's name and received an evasive answer.[56] Once again there was some talk, and the testimonies differ. Throughout the trial, Hiram steadfastly maintained that he didn't know who Larsen was and also that at no time was he told he was being arrested until later on in Spring City.

Glame Bebee. *Author's collection.*

In the starkest, simplest description for this synopsis of the action, Lon Larsen took Hiram by the arm, in a hammerlock position, and forced him out of the beer parlor. The two men proceeded down the street to where Millett's pickup truck was parked, basically in front of the Lorraine Beck Barber Shop. Hiram stated that Larsen punched him in the back periodically during the march. Millett was following them, asking why Hiram was being treated in such fashion. Hiram later testified that Larsen picked him up bodily and threw him in the cab of the truck; Millett ran to get Mrs. Bebee.

Returning with Mrs. Bebee, the two found Hiram in the truck and Larsen either outside the truck totally or reaching into the truck (through the open passenger-side door) abusing Hiram. Larsen either backed away from bending inside the cab of the truck or turned to step to the sidewalk to address Glame Bebee, who asked him what he was doing to her husband. The testimonies differ as to whether Larsen was shot the first time while he was on the sidewalk about to address Glame Bebee or whether he had turned back toward the truck (at the same time reaching for a back pocket) when Hiram fired the first shot. Larsen fell to the pavement, struggling. Hiram stepped out from the truck, looked at Larsen and fired the second shot. Hiram later testified that the second shot was to "help him over the hump."[57]

The three got into the truck and drive a slightly roundabout way back to their residence in Spring City. They were stopped once in route at a crossroads by a man who questioned them briefly, unsuccessfully tried to take their keys and then allowed them to continue on.

They arrived home and were there only a few minutes when the county sheriff and a posse arrived and stormed the house. During the arrest phase of the trial, it came out that there were far more people present than the law officers, estimates of twenty on up to fifty, many of whom made comments that can only be taken as threatening. It was a poorly managed event in terms of crowd control. Mob action was a very real possibility. There was a brief scuffle to do with Hiram surrendering his pistol, and then all of the residents in the house were taken to Manti, the county seat, to be jailed.

GUNSLINGING 101

From the transcript upon cross-examination by Frandsen comes the following:

> Q. Mr. Bebee will you stand and show how you had your arm and the gun pointed when you fired the second shot? A. Sure. You mean just the point of it or draw the gun and show it, which? Q. Just what position you had it when you pulled the trigger. A. I had it in approximately that position. Q. Was that when you fired the fatal shot? A. Yes, sir, the first. Q. How was it when you fired the second shot? A. The only distinction was that I walked over here and pushed the slug about in the left arm there. Q. Did you have your arm extended or was it—was your elbow bent? A. Specifically speaking, I never use a gun that way, I just done that for your benefit. I would leave my wrist loose. Q. You left it loose? A. Loose, relaxed here. Q. Why do you leave it loose? A. Simply to lift it that way. I don't grab it that way. I don't get a collar and elbow hold. Q. You leave it loose so that you can get a better aim with the gun, is that it? A. There is a certain amount of buck in a gun if you understand and I allow for that buck. Q. You found out that a gun has that characteristic through years of experience did you? A. Every one I ever handled has a recoil to a certain extent. Q. And when you shoot you allow for that recoil? A. Yes, as much as possible. Force of habit.

In another exchange, he addressed what one does in a confrontational atmosphere when the other party reaches for his hip pocket: "It is a breach of ettiquette."[58]

VIEWED IN THE PRESENT

Little was said in the trial regarding self-defense. Much more was made of whether the second shot mattered at all, as the first shot was deemed a fatal one. I do not find a single use of the word *fear* being brought in as justification. That is very odd and was a major point for Mother. Hiram was old and frail. On his best day and stretching almost to tiptoes, he barely measured five foot, three inches and weighed only slightly more than one hundred pounds. Lon Larsen was in his prime—thirty-plus years younger than Hiram, bigger and stronger—and he was mad at Hiram. Previously, Hiram had been severely beaten a few times. Until the pistol was drawn, it was Hiram Bebee that was in danger—not Lon Larsen.

After some seven decades have passed, a modern-day crime investigator would be appalled at the record of the handling back in 1945; it was primitive. In some respects, you could say that it was handled on the cheap. Some of the evidence handling can probably be chalked up to the local law enforcement considering it a slam-dunk case; officers did not see into the future of two trials and multiple appeals. At the time of the incident, the people of Sanpete County, law enforcement and general populace were not looking at Hiram Bebee as possibly being the Sundance Kid. Had that been the view, I am sure the case would have had much tighter handling. The reality of the time was that he was an outsider with strange beliefs and a dogmatic manner—people wanted him and his group to leave the county.

A FRIEND'S VIEW

Now here's a totally different perspective from the other side. Hiram Bebee was an amazing man in his own right, a man of high intellectual capacity. This is what my mother and grandfather saw and knew. It was also verified by Justice James Wolfe of the Utah Supreme Court.[59]

Just out of business college, my mother went to work for Paramhansa Yogananda in Los Angeles. He was the author of *Autobiography of a Yogi* and the founder of the Self Realization Fellowship. It was from this relationship that Mother recognized pieces of Vedanta philosophy that were in Hiram Bebee's lessons. My grandfather had been active in Utah politics and the labor movement of 1910 on through the Great Depression. He perhaps did not exactly agree with Hiram Bebee's views on politics and government, but he recognized someone who had studied and thought a great deal about these issues.

Mother and Grandpa Alf were more pragmatic; they could live with commutation down to life in prison, and that is what happened, but only by a hair's breadth. At the November 1948 Board of Pardons meeting, it came out that four of the jurors from the Price trial had been wrestling with their consciences. They had changed their votes in the deliberation process on the understanding that their recommendation for leniency would be adhered to—it was not. Judge Keller had sentenced Hiram to execution, and these four jurors had been agonizing over this reversal of their intention for the following five months until they came forward. A petition had been circulated, getting a wide range of sympathetic signers on board. Three members of the Utah State Bar joined forces and voiced their opinions; one of these, Willard Hanson, had been practicing law since at least 1912, when he had helped on a case brought against my grandfather. The Board of Pardons decided that commutation would be the more judicial choice.

If Hiram were alive and in good health today, what would we see and hear? Even though the rural West has lost most of its insularity with the coming of television and the interstate highway system, he likely would still be a little bit the outsider. In 1945, religious difference was a large part of the ostracism. Hiram had told my mother that his mother was East Indian; that would bring a large measure of plausibility to the decidedly eastern flavor of his teachings and philosophies. Today, some branches of yoga are quite accepted even here. That would mellow both sides considerably.

Computers were barely being dreamed about in 1945 and had only made a few timid steps forward by 1955, when Hiram passed out of the body. It is anyone's guess how he would feel about mobile devices. Whether he used the technology or not, I am sure he would express his views about myriad topics just as he had in the past. If he did take to the technology, he would have a very large and active blog. Where I think he would still be a bit of an outsider is that he would speak out about the ills and flaws he saw. The topics would be wide-ranging, from partitions and international peacekeeping to healthcare and banking and more.

Glame Bebee was a testament to faithfulness. She visited Hiram in prison weekly, with only a few exceptions, until her death in 1953. She died on the steps of the prison administration building as she was entering for her regular visit.[60] We had moved out of state in 1948, so Mother was only able to visit sporadically, but she wrote regularly to Hiram until his death in 1955. Frank O'Bannion was the last of the people in the house in Spring City that night in October 1945; he died in Missouri at the home of his daughter in 1958 or '59. Hiram and Glame were childless. He did not speak of having any relatives; Glame, at the time of her father's death, had been listed as having two sisters, but she did not speak of them to Mother. My mother continued with her clipping file until her own death in 2004. I believe I am the last in the line of "followers" defending Hiram. E. Leroy Shields's daughter-in-law, Shirlee Hurst Shields, authored a screenplay on the trials that was produced in the 1990s. She is still living and adheres to the Sundance Kid allegation. Whether you believe in reincarnation or not, Hiram Bebee (aka George Hanlon and who knows who else) still lives on in the record of the West.

CHAPTER 6
ZANE GREY'S GHOST

BY ED MEYER

Every year during Kanab's Western Legends Roundup, I walk down
Main Street reading the plaques honoring individuals who have
contributed to Kane County's long heritage of western movies. On these
occasions, I'm never alone. Walking beside me, unseen by others, is the ghost
of Zane Grey, whispering, "Have they put up a plaque for me yet? Don't
they know what I did?" And every year, my response disappoints the great
writer's ethereal apparition. Perhaps he will go away if I tell his story and he
is, at last, honored.

OVERVIEW

In mid-April 1907, Zane Grey crossed the Colorado River at Lee's Ferry. He
was a thirty-five-year-old disenchanted dentist and struggling author. When
he stepped off the ferry, he entered a world filled with inspiring panoramas
and an unfamiliar culture dominated by members of the Church of Jesus
Christ of Latter-day Saints (the Mormons).

Although Utah had become a state in 1896, the boundary between Utah
and the Arizona Territory was, for all practical purposes, invisible. Spiritually,
Kane County, Utah, and areas north of the Colorado River known today as
the Arizona Strip were included within a Mormon ecclesiastical unit known
as the Kanab Stake in Zion. (For simplicity's sake, this chapter will identify

Upper crossing at Lee's Ferry on the Colorado, where Grey first stepped onto the Utah-Arizona Strip. *Kathy Meyer Collection.*

this entire area as the "Utah-Arizona Strip"). This area also constituted a cohesive economic unit within which cowboys, shepherds, loggers and miners moved across state lines to earn their livings. To a large extent, this situation continues today.

By the time Zane Grey died thirty-two years later, he was the most published author in the world. He owed much of his success to his friends along the Utah-Arizona Strip who mentored him in 1907 and 1908.

QUICK FACTS

Zane Grey's contribution to literature and film is perhaps best summarized by Dr. Joe Wheeler, co-founder of Zane Grey's West Society:

> *Zane Grey, the Western writer, shaped the way the world will forever perceive the "Old West." Zane Grey's name on theater marquees was a bigger draw than the top Hollywood stars of his day. In 57 novels, 10 books of Western nonfiction, and 130 movies, Grey, who died in 1939 at age 67, almost single-handedly created the "Myth of the*

West." His respectful treatment of Indians was ahead of its time; his word paintings of some of the world's most spectacular country may never be equaled.[61]

Of specific interest to those living on the Utah-Arizona Strip is that sixteen of Grey's works were inspired entirely or partially by locations in their backyard.[62] These works include *Heritage of the Desert, Arizona Ames, Nevada, Last of the Plainsmen, The Young Lion Hunter, Riders of the Purple Sage, Wildfire, The Ranger, Tales of Lonely Trails, Roping Lions in the Grand Canyon, Forlorn River, Wild Horse Mesa, Don—The Story of a Lion Dog, Robber's Roost, The Deer Stalker* and *The Ranger and Other Stories.*[63]

The inspiration for these works include Lee's Ferry, House Rock Valley, the Kaibab National Forest, the North Rim of the Grand Canyon, Fredonia, Kanab, Moccasin, Pipe Springs, the Hurricane Bluffs, Mount Trumbull and the Kaiparowits Plateau.[64]

Of special interest to the board members of Kanab's Western Legends Roundup and fans of cowboy films everywhere is the role that Zane Grey's works played in introducing the world to the Old West through movies. Well over one hundred movies were based on his books,[65] with the following movies filmed partially or entirely on the Utah-Arizona Strip: *Western Union* (Kanab and House Rock Canyon), *The Dude Ranger* (Eagle Rock, Johnson Canyon), *Red Canyon* (Kanab Movie Ranch, Kanab, Paria) and *Heritage of the Desert* (Lee's Ferry).[66]

Perhaps Zane Grey's greatest contribution to the Utah-Arizona Strip's movie heritage was his crusade for

Zane Grey's *Heritage of the Desert. Harper & Brothers New York, 1910.*

movies based on his novels to be shot on location during a time when many, if not most, cowboy movies were shot at the film industry's western movies sets at Lone Pine, California. His efforts played a major role in introducing Utah and northern Arizona landscapes to the movies.[67]

SOLVING ZANE GREY'S MYSTERIES

Zane Grey's earliest visits to the Utah-Arizona Strip were in 1907 and then again in 1908. At that time, he had not yet written any of the western romance novels that would make him famous. His experience on these trips lit the fire for the rest of his literary career.

Grey kept a detailed record of his trips and incorporated his experiences into many of his future works. Several books have been written about his history. Two works that are particularly insightful are *Dolly and Zane Grey: Letters from a Marriage*,[68] edited by Candace C. Kant, and *Zane Grey: His Life, His Adventures, His Women*,[69] by Thomas H. Pauly. The purpose of this chapter, though, is not to parrot the good work of these and other writers.

However, the great writer's adventures on the Utah-Arizona Strip took place over a century ago, and time has obscured the answers to many lingering questions about Grey's visits. These mysteries are worth exploring for two reasons. First, if we solve these mysteries, we will be able to supplement the research that has already been done by Zane Grey scholars. Secondly, the descendants of those who mentored Grey during those early visits will learn of their

Frontispiece by Douglas Duer from *Riders of the Purple Sage* (1912). "Don't look back!"

ancestors' contributions, hidden for so long in family memoirs and oral histories. The walls of places he visited whisper secrets as well.

The remainder of this chapter tries to answer questions about Grey's early visits through a look at two of his most famous novels. The first is *Riders of the Purple Sage*, perhaps the most famous western novel ever written. The second is *Heritage of the Desert*, Grey's first western romance novel and one that set his huge literary success in motion.

Was Riders of the Purple Sage *Originally Set on the Utah-Arizona Strip?*

During the 2012 National Book Festival held on the National Mall on September 22–23, 2012, the Library of Congress released the names of nearly one hundred literary works that were "Books that Shaped America.[70] One of these books was Zane Grey's most famous western romance novel, *Riders of the Purple Sage*. The novel tells the story of a single Mormon woman and a gentile gunfighter who struggle against a Mormon bishop and a wicked

Kane Ranch Cabin on the North Kaibab Ranger District. *U.S. Forest Service, Southwestern Region, Kaibab National Forest.*

elder who try to gain control of the heroine's inherited ranch by forcing her into a polygamous marriage.

Perhaps the single most debated issue among Zane Grey fans relates to the actual locations of places mentioned in *Riders of the Purple Sage*. In 1911, Grey hired a guide named Al Doyle, who showed him several spectacular canyons, complete with ancient ruins, near Kayenta, Arizona. Grey himself admitted that one of these canyons was the model for Surprise Valley, a central location in his novel. The problem is that other locations in the novel do not seem to match the area around this valley.

This chapter suggests that Grey employed literary license to "relocate" places he had visited and people he had met on the Strip during two mountain lion hunting adventures in 1907 and 1908 to mesh with his newly anointed Surprise Valley. Not all Zane Grey researchers have bought into this concept, so let's present the case and let the reader decide for himself or herself.

Surprise Valley

We believe Grey pirated the name "Surprise Valley" from a location two hundred miles west in the Grand Canyon. His 1908 trip journal explains that on April 20, 1908, he left a campsite in "the Saddle" and journeyed over

Looking down from Crazy Jug Canyon over the Surprise Valley and Thunder River Country. *Author's collection.*

the rim of the Grand Canyon down into Surprise Valley, returning the same day.[71] The mystery is which valley Grey actually visited. Grey researchers discount the likelihood of the author being inspired by the location identified on maps today as the Grand Canyon's Surprise Valley. Their conclusion would seem to have merit since this location is a high, somewhat arid desert valley, far different from the valley in Grey's novel. However, early maps show Surprise Valley as being located slightly south along the course of Tapeats Creek. It is perhaps significant that the largest spring in all of the Grand Canyon is Tapeats Spring, which gushes an amazing 48 million gallons per day. This is more than double that of Thunder River Springs, located less than one mile away.[72] The following passage by a present-day tour operator provides perspective into why Zane Grey may have first envisioned his Surprise Valley as being in the Grand Canyon: "The huge outpourings of water at Thunder River, Tapeats Spring and Deer Spring have attracted people since prehistoric times…booming streams of crystalline water emerge from mysterious caves to transform the harsh desert of the inner Canyon into impossibly beautiful green oasis' [sic] replete with the music of falling water and cool pools."[73]

THUNDER RIVER

A broad rippling stream flowed toward him, and at the back of the cañon [canyon] *a waterfall burst from a wide rent in the cliff…Straight at the waterfalls the rustlers drove the burros, and straight through the middle, where the water spread into a fleecy, thin film like dissolving smoke. Following closely, the rustlers rode into this white mist, showing in bold black relief for an instant, and then they vanished.*[74]

These words reveal the hideout of Oldring, the outlaw gang leader in *Riders of the Purple Sage*. In the novel, this secret place was within walking distance of Surprise Valley. So what about the new Surprise Valley discovered by Zane Grey in 1911? Where is the waterfall bursting from the canyon wall? The answer is that there isn't one. Did Grey find a similar falls on his 1908 journey to Grand Canyon's Surprise Valley?

Thomas Pauly related the author's description to his wife Dolly of his experience on this trip: "Heartbroken because there was no access to the valley floor, he located a cliff overlook that unfolded to him the lush vegetation and towering walls that made the valley special. A wondrous river sprang from the side of a distant cliff, plunged 2,500 feet, and twisted its way through the center of the valley." After describing that it took an amazing eighteen seconds for a rock he threw over the edge to reach the bottom, he repeated, 'I expect to find my way down there, and some day take you in and camp for a couple of weeks.'"[75]

The waterfalls were at Thunder River, only a few hundred yards from Tapeats Creek, just like the waterfalls in *Riders of the Purple Sage*.

PIPE SPRINGS

The home of Jane Withersteen stood in a circle of cottonwoods, and was a flat, long, red-stone structure with a covered court in the center through which flowed a lively stream of amber colored water. In the massive blocks of stone and heavy timbers and solid doors and shutters showed the hand of a man who had builded [sic] *against pillage and time.*[76]

We are introduced to the Withersteen House, the home of the primary heroine in *Riders of the Purple Sage*, in the first few pages of the novel. We go on to learn of ponds fed by stone-lined canals from the spring that ran though the home and of low, red stone corrals.

While southeastern Utah offers a variety of ranch houses, none comes close to matching the features outlined in the novel. However, there is one structure on the Utah-Arizona Strip that meets every one of the necessary criteria: Windsor Castle, the old fort at Pipe Springs National Monument.

One of the pools at Pipe Springs. *Keith Foss Collection.*

Unfortunately, none of the monument records indicates a visit by Zane Grey, and the author himself does not mention visiting Pipe Springs. Still, the perfect match suggests that he visited there sometime before the novel was written in 1911. If only there were some record of his being in the area.

MOCCASIN

Collier Brand, the father of all this numerous progeny, was a Mormon with four wives. The big house where they lived was old, solid, picturesque, the lower part built of logs, the upper of rough clapboards, with vines growing up the outside stone chimneys. There were many wooden-shuttered windows, and one pretentious window of glass, proudly curtained in white. As this house had four mistresses, it likewise had four separate sections, not one of which communicated with another, and all had to be entered from the outside. In the shade of a wide, low, vine-roofed porch Jane found Brandt's wives entertaining Bishop Dyer.[77]

The hamlet of Moccasin, Arizona, lies downhill from Pipe Springs, a mere seven-minute drive. Similarly, the town of Cottonwoods was located just downhill from Withersteen House. There is a home in Moccasin listed on the National Register of Historic Places and referred to as "the Big House."[78] The home, built in 1875, matches the description of the big ranch house in Grey's imaginary town. At the time of Zane Grey's visits in 1907 and 1908, the home was owned by Jonathan and Lucy Heaton, and most travelers used the Big House as a rest stop, with as many as 110 guests in a month.

While the Big House seems to match the big house in *Riders of the Purple Sage*, the most significant information was found in a tribute to Lucy Heaton, written based on information provided by her daughter, also named Lucy:

Lucy recorded that a number of famous people were entertained by her parents. Zane Grey was there and rode around the surrounding area. I read his book, "Riders of the Purple Sage," from Lucy's big library with shelves all along the long living room wall, except for the fireplace. I always thought he found his inspiration for the title from the pasture east of our fields where we used to turn the milk cows into the tall sagebrush. I have never seen sagebrush as high as a horse in any other place nor sagebrush of that beautiful blue-purple color.[79]

The Big House, Moccasin, Arizona. *Keith Foss Collection.*

The significance of this information, even though dates of Grey's visits are not included, is that it places the author in the Big House and, due to its proximity, Pipe Springs as well.

Esteemed Zane Grey researcher Charles G. Pfeiffer further supported the role of Moccasin when he stated, "I think he [Grey] used the Mormon settlement at what is now known as Pipe Springs National Monument fourteen miles west of Fredonia as the model for Cottonwoods."[80] The name of that settlement is, of course, Moccasin.

Fredonia

The importance of Fredonia is not the town itself, but rather the person Zane Grey visited in 1908 and possibly in 1907 as well. According to Val Jackson, Grey spent many evenings at the Jackson home in Fredonia and Fredonia's Old Travelers Inn talking with his grandmother Estella Jackson, who was innkeeper. He also shared information passed down through Estella's son, Andrew Jackson, in which he says his mother told him that Grey needed a love interest for *Riders of the Purple Sage* and she guessed it was her.[81]

The current owner of the Old Travelers Inn, Bob Whitaker, shared his understanding that Zane Grey stayed downstairs in room 1 for several days in 1907.[82] There are, however, no records to confirm the author's stay.

In addition, Roland Rider, a cowboy who claimed to have ridden with Zane Grey, said, "He was just a young fellow, you know, out in the west for the first time. But when he went down to Fredonia then he got all the history about the Winsor Castle out at Pipe Springs and how all the Mormons kept their polygamous wives out there."[83]

THE CASE HAS BEEN presented for consideration. The Utah-Arizona Strip has its own Surprise Valley, a waterfall coming from the side of a mountain, a ranch house that matches the Withersteen House almost exactly, a Big House very much like the big house in the novel and a woman who claims she was the model for Jane Withersteen—all integral to *Riders of the Purple Sage*. There is evidence that the author had access to all of these resources and more. The area around Kayenta has a "new" Surprise Valley that Zane Grey came to love in 1911, but that's it—just a canyon. Is there any doubt that the Utah-Arizona Strip played a huge role in Grey's vision for *Riders of the Purple Sage*?

The Utah-Arizona Strip and Heritage of the Desert

Zane Grey's first western romance novel, published in 1910, was about a Mormon patriarch forced to choose between the peaceful ways of his religion and violence to protect his family. There is no doubt that this novel, which launched Grey's career, was wholly about life on the Utah-Arizona Strip. Even the characters are based on real residents Grey had met. The most obvious example is the Mormon patriarch August Naab, based on James Simpson Emett, the cowboy who ran Lee's Ferry during Grey's 1907 and 1908 visits.

In reference to Grey's reaction to the success of the novel, Graham St. John Stott stated, "He was thrilled by his achievement. 'I have given to the world the Mormons in a new and better light,' he proudly wrote to a friend, and anyone familiar with contemporary fiction about Utah and the Saints could not help but agree. At the heart of this tribute to the Mormons was Emmett, thinly disguised as the patriarchal August Naab; in a sense it was his novel."[84]

Zane Grey stayed at Emett's Lonely Dell Ranch near Lee's Ferry. *Keith Foss Collection.*

Certainly the red dust of the Utah-Arizona Strip ran in Jim Emett's blood. Prior to being called on a Mormon mission to Lee's Ferry, he had been Kanab's town marshal. He owned ranches in Cave Lakes Canyon, Cottonwood Canyon west of Kanab and Lonely Dell Ranch, as well as a home in Kanab. His two wives by plural marriage, Emma and Millicent, bore six of his fourteen children in Kanab, another three at the Cottonwood Ranch and one in Orderville.[85]

At least three other characters in *Heritage of the Desert* were based on Utah-Arizona Strip residents. These are Snap Naab (August Naab's prodigal son, based on Emett's oldest son, Snap Emett); the villainous cattleman Holderness (a thinly veiled Charlie Dimmick, the foreman of the Bar Z brand and Jim Emett's enemy); and August Naab's loyal son, Dave (based on Dave Rust, the local guide Zane Grey met in 1907).[86] Other members of August Naab's family—specifically George, Judith, Esther, Mother Mary and Mother Rush—were assuredly other members of Emett's family.

Although Grey typically invented names, locations in the novel correspond to well-known locations on the Utah-Arizona Strip. A great example is in the third chapter, entitled "The Trail of the Red Wall," which describes a trip:

FICTIONAL LOCATIONS FROM *HERITAGE OF THE DESERT*	ACTUAL LOCATIONS ON THE UTAH-ARIZONA STRIP
From White Sage[87]	From Kanab
Up the Coconina Trail	Up Forest Road 22 just east of Fredonia
Over Fire Mountain	Over the Kaibab Plateau
Past the Saddle	Past Saddle Mountain
Down the Windy Slope	Down U.S. 89A heading down to House Rock Valley
With the Grand Canon showing ahead	With the Grand Canyon showing ahead
The Painted Desert in the distance	The Painted Desert in the distance
And the Vermillion Cliffs on the left	And the Vermillion Cliffs on the left
Passing Seeping Spring	Passing Jacob's Pool
And Silver Cup Spring	And Emett Spring
Crossing five miles of red sand	Crossing five miles of red sand
Before arriving at August Naab's "oasis"[88]	Before arriving at Jim Emett's Lonely Dell Ranch

It is also worth noting that the ninth chapter, "The Scent of Desert-Water," is a fictionalize account of an actual event involving sheep stampeding off a cliff to get to water at Cathedral Wash,[89] and the sixteenth chapter, "Thunder River,"[90] was inspired by Grey's 1908 ride into Surprise Valley and Thunder River.[91]

The only true "mystery" is the identity of White Sage and, specifically, the home of Bishop Cole, a Mormon who reluctantly houses a young man, John Hare, found along the road. One possible location is a home in Kanab now called the Purple Sage Inn, known as the Cole Hotel in 1907 and 1908 when Grey visited. Significantly, one of the early scenes in *Heritage of the Desert* is at Bishop Cole's home. Alice Brown, a past owner of the home, said that Zane Grey's son, Loren Grey, told her that he knew his father stayed at the Cole Hotel.[92] This information suggests that Bishop Cole's home was inspired by the Cole Hotel. If so, a logical conclusion is that Kanab is White Sage.

Purple Sage Inn in Kanab, Utah. *Rick Nadolny.*

Conclusion

Riders of the Purple Sage and *Heritage of the Desert* are only two of the novels involving locations, characters and events from along the Utah-Arizona Strip. Each of the other works would have similar examples connecting the book to the local area. In the interest of brevity, I haven't shared oral traditions about cowboys fistfighting with Grey, a cave where the author camped with those same cowboys and much more. However, hopefully enough information has been shared that I will soon see a Western Legends plaque in Zane Grey's honor. Perhaps then the great author's ghost can finally rest.

CHAPTER 7

THE MAGICAL STORY OF MAUDE ADAMS

BY JAMES NELSON

If you sprinkle some magic dust in the air and punch a ticket with Peter Pan to Neverland, you can take a mysterious ride to yesterday and meet a once world-famous movie star who has all but disappeared from public view.

Once upon a time in Salt Lake City, a little baby was plucked from her cradle and promptly delivered to center stage. It was the beginning of the marvelous career of Maude Adams. Early in the twentieth century, she was among the best performers in the world. She made $1 million per year and played the biggest stages in New York City and around the country.

It all started at the Brigham Young Theatre in downtown Salt Lake City, where actress Annie Kiskadden performed and often allowed her baby, Maude, to be held just off stage. Annie was the female lead in *The Lost Baby*. The play called for a baby to be brought out on a silver platter. During one of the performances, the baby normally used for the role pitched a fit and would not cooperate. The stage manager looked around and spotted baby Maude. It seemed a natural replacement, and it worked. Little Maude reportedly sat up on the platter and made eye contact with the audience like only babies can do, and this prompted laughter throughout the theater. A new star twinkled that evening that started an incredible trajectory.

Maude was born on November 11, 1872, to James Henry Kiskadden and Asaneth Ann Adams. Mormon pioneer ancestry came through her mothers' side and, from her father, the "gentile" side, as Maude would say. The Mormons learned early on about the value of not only hard work but also entertainment and recreation.

MAUDE ADAMS IN HER FOUR EARLIEST ROLES
REPRODUCTIONS FROM RARE PRINTS LOANED "THE STAR" BY C. L. RITZMANN, THE COLLECTOR.

Maude Adams as a child. *From the* New York Star, *January 9, 1909.*

MORMON HERITAGE

Maude Adams came from that gritty pioneer stock. Her grandfather Barnabas Adams worked as a night guard tending to cattle out on the trail while Brigham Young and the pioneers slept. It was those pioneers, the Mormons, who brought with them music, theater and entertainment along with their wagons, recipes and Bibles. In the churches, hotels, bowries, dance halls and saloons, they sang, danced and acted every play they knew, including Shakespeare. Those are the roots of Maude Adams.

"These people literally sing, dance and recreate across the plains to lift their spirit," said history tour guide Mary Ellen Elggren. "Brigham Young saw this as a very important thing, and he had a basic philosophy that, in life, to be a well-developed, well-rounded person, you slept eight hours, you worked eight hours and you recreated eight hours…So, how do you fill up eight hours of recreation a day in the life of a member of the LDS church? There are lots of ways. It was active participation, but certainly dancing and theater played a big role in filling up that space of time in every member's life," added Elggren.

May Blayney and Maude Adams in *Chantecleer*. *Bain News Service, via Wikimedia Commons.*

At age four, Maude was in San Francisco with her mother learning all aspects of the theater industry. She toured around the western United States with her mother and adopted her mother's maiden name for her stage billing. Maude grew up, and the acting roles came calling. Among the many plays Adams starred in include *Lord Chumley*, *The Masked Ball*, *The Little Minister*, *Romeo and Juliet*, *A Kiss for Cinderella* and *Quality Street*.

PETER PAN

The entertainment star system a century or so ago meant that a few people commanded a lot of respect and power. One of those people was Charles Frohman. Frohman started out as newsboy and then got into big-city newspaper work and, finally, theater management. He seemed destined to shuffle the Broadway plays of the day like a deck of cards. He dealt the winning hand frequently, and actors clamored to be under his tutelage. Frohman bought the rights to a work by playwright James Mathew Barrie in 1905. He pointed to Maude Adams for the starring role. *Peter Pan* was a booming success on stage. It was a bold move that paid a fortune to the inner circle.

"The great playwright J.M. Barrie wrote the stage production of his most famous play, *Peter Pan*, for Maude Adams to star in because he was smitten with her, like every other male who ever set eyes on her," said historian and rare book expert Ken Sanders. Sanders knows the story of Maude Adams well and has books, photos and artifacts relating to the Utah-born stage star. "The part was written for her. This is where, in all of theater, this role of women playing men's roles came from. From Barrie writing the Peter Pan role for Adams, and that's a tradition that is alive and well in the theater today," said Sanders.

PLAYING TO THE HOME CROWD

In search of her story, we wondered if Maude Adams might have played in Fairview, Manti, Mount Pleasant, Moroni or any other central Utah towns. There were endless possibilities to which the most prolific stage star might have ventured along Utah back roads and played stage dates. Research does show that Maude played at a small theater in Corrinne, Utah, but that is way north. We were curious about the historic corridor in the middle of the state. We heard whispers and stories that it happened. Perhaps she acted in a weekend performance of *Romeo and Juliet* in Mount Pleasant or Manti. Maybe she took the train down to Panguitch to thrill locals with her signature role. We traveled along the Mormon Pioneer National Heritage Area (MPNHA) over a number of months to learn more. We met with people in diners, on horseback, on their sheep ranches and on their front porches. The beautiful Moroni Opera House seemed like a logical place to check out. Standing proudly on the edge of town, the opera house was built with native brick and stone in 1891. You won't find an older public building in the community. The opera house has been restored and is busy year-round, hosting cultural and social events. Inside the building, we met with Utah storyteller and musician Clive Romney about the Maude Adams theory.

"Utah can be very proud of the fact that Maude Adams was a local girl who not only made good but in her time became the most famous actress of all," said Clive Romney. "Yes. That much we do know, but did she ever play down here, in this opera house or maybe down the road?" we asked. "Rumor has it, some people think she acted here in Sanpete County on one or more of these stages. We have no proof of that. She might have gone underground, but it is an interesting possibility that Maude Adams—the highest-paid actress in the world at that time—might have come back home and acted here," said a smiling Romney. Despite strong theater and music history all along this historic corridor, no one could provide evidence that Adams ever played down here. Most people we asked had never even heard of her. We could find no connection of her playing the Moroni Opera House.

In the town of Fairview, just up the street from the old Corner Station store that once fueled cars and trucks rumbling along Highway 89, we found another possible theater clue: the Lionel L. and Clista Lasson Peterson Dance Hall. We discovered that the old dance hall has been restored so families can hold reunions and wedding parties inside. School theater productions thrive on stage, and countless community events are held on the beautiful, polished hardwood floors. It seems like a perfect place to have hosted a night with Adams on stage. The dance hall would have been a logical place for a grande dame of the stage to play for locals. Indeed, it was a popular place during the era when Maude was around. After knocking on doors and exhausting all tips and clues, we found nothing concrete. No one could vouch that she ever stepped onto the stage to act or perform in this town. Curtain closed.

Down the road a few miles in Spring City, Utah, the buildings, yards and the roads are organized just like they were a century ago. Sturdy brick homes,

Actress Maude Adams, circa 1898. *Library of Congress.*

sweeping shade trees, wood corrals and quiet streets. Lots of pioneer families lived here, and many were polygamist families. History, culture and heritage thrive in this town. The entire community is on the National Register of Historic Places. Today, all sorts of artists call this community home. Painters, musicians, sculptors, singers and dancers often converge on Main Street in Victory Hall. It's a quaint little theater that goes back to the time when Maude Adams was in her prime.

That's where local historian Woody Challis showed posters, photos and literature about Maude Adams. He then responded to questions about whether or not she might have played in any of the local stage productions. "Victory Hall…this is it, a great venue for what we are looking at." We noted, "Entertainment, theater, historic elements and, of course, Maude Adams…we're trying to find out the whole story, Woody. We still don't have everything."

Challis said, "With all the information we've got on Maude, we still don't know if she acted in one of these southern Utah theaters." We replied, "[They] dotted the entire area, it was common to have the theaters, and they played. It was the big thing then." Indeed it was, he responded. "There has been an element in the culture of these people that settled this area. The Mormon culture from the Kirtland period. It's an amazing thing," said Challis.

Although we had little success finding places in Utah where Adams might have performed, we easily found out that she kept strong ties to her home. Utah ties to Adams are sprinkled throughout her amazing career. In 1909, she provided tickets for the touring Mormon Tabernacle Choir to see her onstage in New York City. The play was *Peter Pan*, and after it was over, everyone stood up and sang "Auld Lang Syne." Imagine that scene.

In the Movies

Maude Adams was famous a long time ago, but few people today know of her fame and fortune. There is plenty of history on Adams if you dig into the archives and search her career. Somehow she has slipped from the bright lights and center stage. Her stage career was marvelous and undoubtedly was considered among the best in the business. As the motion picture industry began crowding into the entertainment picture, Maude began seeing that she was on the last act of her own career. While she dabbled in conversations about being in movies, it never happened. Some reports indicate that she saw a filmed screen test, and that that was enough. She decided that it was time to move on in life.

"It's a fascinating story, you know. Here in the twenty-first century, seemingly, hardly anybody remembers who Maude Adams is or was. Back in her day, she was one of the most famous actresses in the world. She was as famous as Sarah Bernhardt, who everyone still has heard of. But Maude Adams, not so much," said Sanders.

In 1980, the romantic film *Somewhere in Time* was released starring Christopher Reeves and Jane Seymour. The movie was based on a book written about the life of Maude Adams. Each year at the Grand Hotel on Mackinac Island in Lake Michigan, an amazing thing happens that connects people to the romantic movie. Fans dress in early 1900s clothing, listen to lectures and screen the movie they love so much. The legacy of the movie and all of its history attract international interest. It's also another way the mystery of Maude Adams continues. The movie was based on the 1975 novel *Bid Time Return* by Richard Matheson. The main character is tailored after Adams. Historians say that Matheson was struck by a portrait of Adams hanging on a wall in a Virginia City, Nevada opera house. He studied her work and life and found enough material to fill his book and thus the movie. Today, fans of the film circle a date each fall for their gathering and celebrate the story. There's even an official Somewhere in Time website with an international chapter. Jewelry, photos, posters, DVDs, clothing and other collectibles are available.

PLAYING IT FORWARD

Maude did exit the stage for a number of years and stayed away from publicity of any sort. Then Stephens College in Missouri asked her to teach on its all-girls campus. In researching one of our *Discovery Road* documentary programs for the Mormon Pioneer National Heritage Area (MPNHA), we found a rare recording of this step in Maude's life. It was fortuitous to be able to hear her voice and gain further insight to this enigma. On a National Broadcasting Company radio program in 1937, Maude was introduced as someone dearly loved across the country.

Radio announcer Durward Kirby welcomed the star and allowed her a chance to set the stage for this new chapter in her life: "Tonight the National

Broadcasting Company presents a special program from the campus of Stephens College. One of the oldest colleges for women in the middle west at Columbia, Missouri," exhorted Kirby to the radio audience. He then described the college's plan to improve education and the bold step to bring someone special to the Missouri campus: "The introduction on his campus of one of America's best-known actresses as an instructor. The actress, well, you need no introduction, for the memory of *Peter Pan* will long live in this land of ours. Tonight at my side is Miss Maude Adams. Miss Adams left the seclusion of retirement, which she has maintained with but few interruptions for the past several years, to head the drama department at Stephens."

Kirby then teased the listeners with a promise that Miss Adams will answer the question of why she came out of retirement to teach drama classes. Song and dramatization, including some dedicated to the *Peter Pan* story, followed the national broadcast before Maude stepped to the microphone. The old recording has just a brief moment of popping and static before her voice starts. Her response is in reference to the Stephens College president inviting her to teach in a new way:

> *I saw that it was not at all a conventional school of acting that he had in mind but something which would relate theater and acting to the emotions of everyday life. This idea came very near a long held belief of my own, that we should know more about our emotions and have greater faith in them, greater respect for them. They're the finest things we have. Because of this opportunity, I've re-entered the theater through another door; working with these sincere young women confirms me in the belief that the theater will always influence human creatures and hold her place in the realm of the spirit of man.*

The old recording gave sound to the countless Maude Adams theater photos out there. Her voice was sophisticated and classy, each word measured with emotion fitting for the event. Her years at Stephens College (between 1937 and 1943) appeared to fill a void in her life away from the spotlight. The students had missed the heyday of her career but certainly benefited from her vast talent and knowledge of theater. Away from teaching, she tinkered with ideas on improving theater lighting for a time but mostly stayed out public view. "Maude Adams was her own woman and did things her way and clearly by the end of her life was very, very successful, [as she] left a sizeable fortune to a covenant of nuns back on the East Coast, and I don't think she ever had any regrets about her life," said Sanders.

Miss Maude Adams, performing arts poster, from photo by Aim Dupont. Created by the Strobridge Lith Company, Cincinnati and New York, 1899. *Library of Congress.*

Maude certainly had accomplished fame and fortune. She also managed to keep people guessing about who she really was off stage. Local newspapers often pondered the mystery of the stage star, as did national periodicals like the *New York Times*, which noted on March 1, 1914, "The legends that have grown up about Maude Adams are without end. She is the most guessed about person in stage life."

Time passed, and the allure of Maude Adams faded measurably. She died in seclusion in Upstate New York at age eighty. Mayor Mansfield Showers told the *Schenectady Gazette* on July 18, 1953, that she was all but forgotten by then: "Sometimes when you'd mention her to someone, they'd ask, 'Who's Maude Adams?' People forget."

Elusive History

In the Daughters of the Utah Pioneers Museum in Salt Lake City, there are some intriguing pieces of the Maude Adams story. On the main floor, just inside a massive entryway adorned with a century-old, green- and gold-trimmed curtain from the Salt Lake Theater is a dimly lit room of dramatic artifacts. There's a rickety section of old theater seats, tattered playbills, faded show tickets, black-and-white photographs and opera glasses once used to follow the stage action. You can also see a nondescript, rough-hewn baby cradle, long ago a home to baby Maude. In a darkened corner, a hard-to-see framed poster of the actress hangs alone and forgotten. The story of the most famous actress of her day, someone who raked in $1 million per year, is an obscure footnote in history.

The magical story of Maude Adams seems unreal, like it never truly happened. You can Google her name and read the accounts of her fame and fortune. You can scroll through the endless photos of her in those many stage roles and imagine her thrilling the packed auditorium, theaters and stages. Still, though, she eludes us. She did so much but remains hidden from full public view. Her last act might be floating effortlessly from us in a friendly game of hide-and-seek. In this quiet museum setting, where real-life historical events are housed, you can unleash your imagination. Visualize a packed theater more than a century ago. The audience is abuzz with anticipation at the curtain opening. Then the house lights go down, the curtain slowly opens and a spotlight arcs wide and then downward to center stage. Squeeze your eyes tightly shut now and think of Peter Pan! There she is, right there in colorful costume and in full view of our mind's eye, chasing the wind and dancing with sparkling fairy dust.

Maude Adams is in Neverland. Right where she belongs.

CHAPTER 8

HANS ULRICH BRYNER JR.

BY JACK MONNETT

I came to Brigham Young University after joining the Mormon Church and assumed that I was the first member of my family to become a "Utah Mormon." While on my first pilgrimage to Temple Square in Salt Lake City, I was startled to see the first cabin built in the original Salt Lake Fort by Osmyn Deuel. "Deuel," a somewhat unusual name, was my mother's maiden name, and I wondered at the connection. Sure enough, an uncle in the 1830s had built the cabin and later founded the city of Centerville (originally Deuel Creek) just a few miles north. I was more Mormon than I knew.

Then, a few years ago, I attended an education conference. Amid the chatting between lectures, I overheard two women talking. Referring to the film *Seventeen Miracles*, one said to the other, "I really wish that the 18th miracle had been part of the movie—Hans Ulrich Bryner Jr." That caught my attention. Hans Ulrich Bryner was part of my ancestry also—a progenitor of my stepfather to whom I had been sealed. I knew little about Ulrich. I had seen the graveside monument in St. George to Hans Ulrich Bryner Sr., the first person buried there, but aside from that, I only had snippets of Bryner information. In fact, I wasn't really sure about the father and the son—the father who was interred in St. George and the blind son who became a pioneer legend.

Receiving some information at that time, I immersed myself in the son's life—an impossible life by today's standards. His parents, the senior Ulrich and Verena Wintsch, were fairly well-off shoemakers in nineteenth-century Switzerland. Ulrich Jr. was born in Illnau, Zurich, Switzerland, in 1827 and,

Osmyn Deuel Log Cabin, Temple Square (moved from original site), Salt Lake City, Salt Lake County, Utah. Historic American Buildings Survey, John P. O'Neill, photographer, February 20, 1937. *Library of Congress.*

Centerville Deuel House. *Tricia Simpson (own work)* [CC BY-SA 3.0] *via Wikimedia Commons.*

like his parents, appeared to also be on the road to a successful life. Ulrich's early years were spent in his father's trade and in farming. At the same time, he excelled in schoolwork and was proficient in at least five languages.

At sixteen, Ulrich and a close friend became quite ill. His friend died, and Ulrich feared that he would also. While recovering, he experienced a vivid, never-to-be-forgotten dream that he shared with his family. His granddaughter Lura Redd described the dream:

> *A man came to him, took him by the hand and led him in darkness half way around the world. He was in total darkness so that he saw nothing until they came to the top of the world. Then the heavens opened above their heads and he saw a bright light come down and he saw the City of Zion. Its loveliness was above description. He saw a big wall with three gates leading through it and righteous and holy people were going through them into the city. He also wanted to go through the gates into the city but the guide held his hand before him and said, 'You can't go through now but if you are faithful and true, the time will come when you are allowed in." It was at this juncture that he began to notice the man who was leading him—he had grey whiskers and very peculiar eyes.*[93]

Members of his family were interested, but none could interpret it. Only later would Ulrich learn that the overwhelming darkness would be blindness. Finally mending from his sickness, he entered the trade of butchering and specialized in hog killing, including scalding, scraping, hanging and drawing hogs. As in other pursuits, he excelled and shortly had garnered four prize cups. Because of his butchering skill and adeptness at foreign languages, he was named slaughtering house superintendent and chief buyer.

While at work, Ulrich attempted a new personal best time in hog preparation. This time, however, the foot of the hog slipped from its securing cross pin and split Ulrich's pupil. When Ulrich cried out, his younger brother, Casper, wrestled him free from the hog that had fallen on top of him. His eye hung from its socket, and Ulrich repeated, "I am blind! I am blind!" While convalescing, a fever caused him to become blind in his other eye also.

During his recuperation, he often confided in his wife, Maria. While conversing one day, Maria's mother entered the room and said prophetically, "You can do nothing but pray about it and maybe the Lord will open a way for you. I believe the hand of the Lord is in it for a whispering voice says to me, 'Don't feel sorry that Bryner is blind, he is not left. It's good for you but you don't know it yet.'"[94] Four months later, following his grueling recovery, Ulrich was given another vision:

> *I found myself in a great dark room with no glimmer of light. Three fires appeared each of a different size. I turned my eyes and beheld a man who stood at my side. I looked into his face and his size, his grey whiskers, and his peculiar eyes. He was the same man I had seen who had led me half way around the world before. He had an open book in his hand that I had not seen before. He crossed out my sins from the book and they fell to the floor. A voice said to me, "You will have to go through the middle fire"; and I said, "I am able to go through, I am able to stand that, too." Then the wall cracked open so wide that we were able to go through. The light was as bright as the sun at noon and the road to Zion was shown to me. To get there we would cross the sea with a great company. I had my wife and children and it was a long journey. I think that the great prairie into the mountains was the same place that I had seen before.*[95]

So much hinged on the stranger with the "peculiar eyes." Soon Ulrich heard that two Americans were in town teaching about Mormonism, and Maria was sent to listen, to see if one of them had the strange eyes seen in his vision. Maria related that one, Elder George Meyer, was very cross-eyed and wore extremely thick lenses. That was the sought-after description.

Believing the new gospel, Ulrich was the first baptized of twelve in the Bryner and Mathys families (the latter his in-laws). In early January 1855, a ship left with twenty-one-year-old Casper; Ulrich's sister, Barbara; and his brother-in-law, John Mathys—the first of the Swiss immigrants setting out for Utah. It was decided that Ulrich would follow the next year, with Casper already having paved the way for the family. From St. Louis, following an outbreak of cholera that left forty of the immigrants dead, Casper and his family experienced a relatively easy trip into Lehi, Utah.

One year later, however, the journey was not as pleasant for Ulrich. Upon arriving in America, Ulrich was assigned to the John A. Hunt ox-driven wagon train and began the journey from Council Bluffs, Iowa, to the Great Salt Lake. Hunt's company and another wagon train, led by William B. Hodgett, closely followed the ill-fated Martin and Willie handcart companies of 1856, with instructions to give aid to any handcart pioneers unable to keep up. Traveling with his wife, mother and five-year-old daughter, Mary, Ulrich helped push his wagon through the overland trek. Just a week after beginning, the wagon train's journal account described the company's first mishap: "While going up a hill toward the road, Brother Bryner's wagon got into a hole and tipped over. His wife, child and mother were in the wagon, but were not badly hurt, although all the bows were smashed."[96]

The bows holding the canvass above the wagon were difficult to repair and, until mended, made the journey challenging both for riding and sleeping. This sign foreshadowed still more trying events that the Bryners would endure. A few weeks later, there was a stampede (an all-too-common hazard), which caused the Bryner wagon to be upset again. An older woman riding with them was sitting on a cast-iron stove, and when the wagon tipped, Mary fell first, the older woman fell on her and then the stove crashed on top of the pair. Protecting Mary as best she could, the older woman soon died from the fall and the stove's heavy weight. Although Mary also suffered significant injury, she lived through the experience. Ulrich later wrote, "We called the Elders and they administered to my child. They said the Lord would not take her from me for she would be my guide for the journey across the plains."[97]

Just two months following the trek's outset, the keeper of the journal account wrote, "Sister Susannah [Verena] Bryner from Switzerland died somewhat suddenly this morning, although she had been declining for sometime past. At 1 o'clock she asked for a drink, and half an hour later she was found dead. This sister, who was buried at 8:00 a.m., was sixty-four years old."[98]

Now, having lost his mother, traveling with his wife and severely hurt daughter and blind, Ulrich continued his journey to Salt Lake City holding

Mormon pioneers about to enter Salt Lake Valley, July 24, 1847. *Library of Congress, circa 1912.*

on to the rear of the oxcart. By October 17, the first frost came. For four months and 1,300 miles, Ulrich walked behind, stumbling, gripping the oxcart and pushing to help through the mud and unusually deep snow. His feet froze while oxen and other pioneers gave up their lives to the weather. In various accounts, many who had started out so late in the year wrote of their limbs freezing, turning black with gangrene and being sawn off with crude instruments and their living maimed for the rest of their lives.[99] Ulrich, however, followed Brigham Young's advice and made a poultice of sage and snow to regularly rub on his frostbitten feet. His limbs were spared. Little Mary was actually frozen stiff while on the trek, but Ulrich rubbed and rubbed until she regained consciousness. After thirty-nine days, the oxcart and handcart companies were forced to halt. Finally reaching Ulrich's company, rescuers wrote:

> The next morning we rode over to the Hunt Camp twelve miles further on and found them almost out of provisions, and their cattle dying for want of food. The majority of them had become so discouraged that they knew not what to do. We explained to them how impossible it was for us to give them substantial aid as we had but nine loads of provisions left which amounted to very little where there were so many to feed. We urged them to move on toward the valley every day no matter what the sacrifice might be. We gave them to understand that the authorities in Salt Lake City had no idea that they were so far from home. The clouds were gathering fast for another storm and just as we were leaving it commenced to snow quite hard.[100]

But the journey was still incomplete. While the immigrant wagons were regrouping, the Hunt Train lingered. In a single night, sixteen pioneers froze to death. On November 11, long after the snow had begun to fall, the beleaguered pioneers saw a shadowy figure haltingly approach them. The man, Ephraim Hanks, explained that three times during the night a voice directed him to take food to the Hunt Company. Limping his way into camp, he brought two horses loaded with buffalo meat and remained a few days to secure many more.[101] Through his help, the Hunt Company reached the Salt Lake Valley on December 15, losing many of their original number along the way.

For Ulrich, trials continued. Handicapped by blindness, recuperating from frostbite, now in a strange place where he had no sense of landmarks and geography and compounded by his lack of understanding English, there was little he could do. Casper had been part of the rescue party to the waylaid saints but had been unable to reach the Hunt Company. Now, believing Ulrich to be in Lehi, Casper labored to find him with his broken English. In descriptive language, he went from tent to tent asking, "Has anyone here seen a blind man?" Finally, he heard that a blind man had taken the northern route through Ogden Canyon and was in Salt Lake City. Casper walked to Salt Lake and again questioned, "Has anyone here seen a blind man?" Finally finding each other, joyful tears fell at their reunion.

Initially, Ulrich and Casper were called to settle in Ogden. Then, four years later, Brigham Young asked them to homestead southern Utah and be numbered with the Dixie pioneers. The unique calling was extended to brew sacrament wine for the church according to Doctrine & Covenants 27:3–4: "You shall not partake of [wine] except it is made new among you." With the calling came Brigham's admonition: "It's about your only way of making a living but you want to be sure to handle the wine and not let the wine handle you."[102] From 1861 to 1884, Ulrich made roughly one thousand gallons of wine annually for the church. While in Dixie, Maria's brother, John Mathys, came to America and joined the Bryner family. Demonstrating the depth of conviction to his new religion, John was responsible for assisting later Swiss immigrants and printing one thousand copies of the Book of Mormon.

Following five years in Dixie, Ulrich moved his family north to New Harmony. Like many of Utah's founders, Ulrich was a polygamist who married women who had lost husbands through harsh settlement experiences. With his first wife, Maria, he fathered eight children. Then he married a widowed Swiss woman, Margaretha Kuhn, who bore him ten more children. Margaretha settled in Toquerville, just twenty miles southeast of New Harmony. Ulrich kept farms in both locations and frequently traveled between them.

But life wasn't easy for a blind man. The first responsibility of all Bryner children was to learn to lead "Grandpa." Blindness did not exempt Ulrich from responsibilities and instead produced various complications. The boys helped him drive horses by placing their hands over his while Ulrich held the reins. Despite the unusual driving, Ulrich maintained a perfect safety record through the steep and rocky terrain.

Oftentimes, when a particular sense is lost, it is compensated by another. In this, Ulrich had special keenness. Many attested that he was able to feel a horse's coat and tell its color. He was skilled at pruning vines and fruit trees and maintaining productive farms. He was especially adept at weaving baskets from willows and made them from touch to equate exactly to peck, half-bushel and bushel sizes. His baskets were sought after as the best in

Inside a covered wagon at the Hole-in-the-Rock Interpretive Center, Escalante, Utah.
Mormon Pioneer National Heritage Area.

the area. He was acutely aware of voices and could recognize those that he hadn't heard in years. Although blind, he continued making shoes and butchering—in fact, it was said that he could butcher an animal as well as any man in the country.

A great blessing to Ulrich was the gift of dreams. He described the Hill Cumorah and wagonloads of revelatory books that he had seen in vision. Then, on his seventy-fifth birthday, he wrote retelling a particularly poignant dream:

> *I saw a man walking along on top of the wheat which was ready for harvesting. I stood still for I saw something stretched while he walked on to meet me. He came and shook hands with me and called me by my name. I said, "How do you know my name?" He answered, "My name is Peter. We all know you."*
>
> *…I walked in our city and a man came to meet me. He shook hands with me and called me by name. "I am Brother Joseph. I know you." A bitter enemy passed by. I saw him go into the house of the police. I said, "That man is going to betray you. Follow me and they shall never catch you."*
>
> *…I studied the gospel and I could preach to the people by day and by night. I know that the Lord was my guide. I sat on my porch and saw Brigham come. He stopped by my gate with his buggy team. I went out and shook hands with him. He said, "How do you do Brother Bryner? I would like to take with you my dinner." I said, "Brother Brigham, you are welcome to come in." I called for my son to unhitch his team. I went to the garden and told my wife to come in. "Brigham is here. He wants to take dinner with us." She said, "Oh, I don't know what to do. I am not ready for that." "Oh," Brigham said, "Chicken pie and cake. I am tired of that every day. Roasted potatoes and buttermilk will suit me best." I said, "Well, come in and get it ready. We have plenty of that."*[103]

In 1884, at fifty-seven, Ulrich was called to relocate to Price, Utah. Although the town would not be officially established for eight more years, he and a few others initiated the settlement. Building Price's first house with timber from the surrounding hills, his home stood in what is now the center of the city. Then, as his earlier vision had so clearly foreshadowed, he was again literally drawn through fire.

On a sweltering summer night, Ulrich and his family slept outside. Then a fire struck. Unable to see its extent, Ulrich was severely burned while rushing into his home to save important papers. Undaunted, his new home was constructed with mortar and rock that he fashioned and compacted.

Above: The Albert and Mariah Bryner House, a historic home in Price, Utah. *Tricia Simpson (own work)* [CC BY-SA 3.0] *via Wikimedia Commons.*

The Bryner family. *Courtesy of Conrad Bryner.*

He brought seeds from St. George and cultivated the first vineyard in Price and also pioneered beekeeping there. Soon he had two homes, and both his wives settled there. Then, although short-lived, he married a third wife, Susanna, but with the sudden fire and subsequent family displacement, she died.

At the age of seventy, Ulrich launched his life's ambition: the pursuit of family history and working in the temple he had helped to build in St. George. Through frugality and some modest wealth, he hired researchers in Switzerland to trace his family roots. Eventually, he was able to compile information on more than five thousand ancestors who had temple work completed in the St. George Temple.

Opposite, bottom: St. George Utah Temple of the Church of Jesus Christ of Latter-day Saints in St. George, Utah. *Photo by Ricardo630, Attribution, Share Alike 2.5 Generic License via Wikimedia Commons.*

Before his death at seventy-eight, Ulrich was able to visit children and grandchildren scattered throughout the territory. On one of those visits to New Harmony, he bore testimony to the little congregation:

> *He thanked the Lord for all of his blessings. He thanked the Lord for taking his eyesight. He said that if he'd have had his eyesight and done what he'd wanted to do, he never would have joined the Church. He never would have come all the way out to Utah and raised his family here in Zion. He never would have had the peace and contentment that living the gospel had brought him. He had lived long enough to realize this. Now he knew that his blindness was a blessing in disguise.*[104]

In 1905, Ulrich was found on his knees in his home in St. George, and it appeared as though he was looking for something on the floor. Instead, he had suffered a massive stroke and collapsed while engaging in his ancestral pursuit. Just as he had agreed when shown the vision of fire, Hans Ulrich Bryner Jr. passed through the fires of adversity. His legacy was one of triumph over pain, handicap and hardship while pursuing his religion—the thing to him of most worth. In the face of adversity and disability, his obedience to the Lord and his prophets was exemplary. No wonder that the apostle Peter, Joseph Smith and Brigham Young would include him among their friends. As Peter had said, "We all know you."

Postscript

A few years ago, I was wandering the roads of New Harmony, imagining life in the previous century. While there, I walked through the old cemetery, where Ulrich knew many who were there. My eyes suddenly found a Deuel family also interred there in the tiny cemetery, and a quickening thrilled me. I wondered at the inspiration that emanated from the unseen world to bring the Deuel and Bryner families together again just two generations later. My mother, a good Episcopalian who had never heard of Mormonism, and my stepfather, Gilbert Bergen Bryner, who was a recovering alcoholic, had met in an Episcopalian church and married in 1954. They were later sealed in the St. George Temple to complete our family circle.

CHAPTER 9
FRONTIER JUSTICE

By Shirley Bahlmann

For as long as mankind has gathered together to live in tribes, hamlets, villages, towns and cities, rules of social conduct have been established to keep the peace. In Moses's time, most people swore by the "eye for an eye" system of justice. By the time America was founded, law was based first on English Common Law and later on the U.S. Constitution.

As pioneers pushed out into the wilds of their vast country, they left behind the legal institutions and structures that once governed them, and this encouraged some to become a law unto themselves.

Complicating things further was the fact that the land they intended to settle was already occupied by a race of people who knew nothing of English Common Law or the U.S. Constitution. These people had their own ideas of what crime was and how justice could be best administered. As a consequence, justice on the far-flung frontiers could be wild and wooly by today's standards, and the concept of justice between white men and American Indians frequently led to misunderstandings and conflict.

Stories in this chapter illustrate how some people tried getting away with crimes in the wilderness that they may never have attempted in a more populated area. Other stories tell how the laws of two cultures sometimes clashed, while others portray a surprising similarity, demonstrating at times a healthy respect from one civilization to the other.

CRIMES AGAINST WOMEN

One point of view that tends to cross boundaries of culture and history is the tendency to generally view females with a lack of respect.

Conrad Frischknecht reported a story told to him by Judge Wooley of Manti, Utah,[105] about a wealthy Sanpete County man identified only as "John" who was tired of his "silly" wife. One day, while traveling through the mountains above Fountain Green, Utah, with his wife and baby daughter, John suddenly stopped on the trail. Perhaps it was his unnamed wife's idea to take a bathroom break, or he may have forced her to get out of the wagon with their child. Whatever the reason, once she and the baby were out, John drove out of the valley and through the town of Fountain Green alone, undoubtedly confident that his silly wife and baby would perish in the wilderness.

Whether he planned this action ahead of time or made a sudden decision along the trail is unknown. Whatever the case, he must have thought that freeing himself of marriage was easier by abandoning his wife and baby girl than enduring the emotional, financial and social upheaval of divorce. His plan failed when his aggrieved wife stumbled into town with her baby clutched in her arms and was saved by the townspeople.

Still determined to rid himself of his wife and child, John doggedly took on the legal system and obtained a divorce in the county court. He thought he was home free, but unfortunately for him, William D. Livingston, a lawyer who eventually went on to be appointed to the judge's bench, took up the mistreated wife's case.

Knowing that a valid divorce had to be processed through a district court, Livingston took legal action against John and won the case. Although the exact amount awarded to his ex-wife in the proceeding is lost in the annals of history, court records show that Mr. Livingston was awarded $10,000 in attorney's fees (worth about $290,000 in 2015 dollars). Assuming that lawyers then earned a similar fee structure as they do today, the $10,000 would represent about one-third of the total award, netting John's ex-wife perhaps as much as $20,000, nearly $600,000 in today's money. Not bad for a time when $500 could buy a fine farm.

ABANDONMENT WAS NOT UNHEARD of in Native American culture either. For some tribes, it was simply a way of life, especially for the elderly.

Jewel King Larsen reported a story from the Samuel Eleazer King history.[106] The King family, with their six daughters and youngest child, a son named Samuel, arrived at Fort Ephraim, Utah, in the spring of 1855. While gathering wood in the foothills, Samuel's father, Eleazer, was startled to find an old Indian woman lying unconscious on the ground. He rescued her and took her back to the fort, only to discover that she had been abandoned by her people, perhaps because she was regarded as too old or sick to contribute to the upkeep of the tribe any longer.

Eleazer and his wife, Mary Caroline, took the old woman in and patiently nursed her back to health. This took a bit of time, during which the elderly Native American woman became fond of the family, especially of Samuel, who was a bright, lively three-year-old. Despite her affection for the King family, when the old woman was well enough to work, she chose to return to the familiarity of life with her tribe.

Young Samuel was instructed to never leave the fort, but the fascination of hopping rabbits was a sore temptation for the toddler. Chasing the funny animals took the little boy so far outside the safety of the fort walls that an Indian brave on horseback galloped in, swooped him up onto his horse and then rode for his village with his screaming trophy. One old Indian woman in his tribe turned toward the familiar cry.

That night, after Samuel had cried himself to sleep and everyone else had settled down for the night, the old woman stole into the kidnapper's teepee, picked up the sleeping Samuel, carried him in her arms all the way back to the fort and placed him in the arms of his grateful parents. It is not known if the old Indian woman's duplicity was discovered by her tribe or whether she got away with carrying out justice for the white man, but the Kings viewed her act as more than enough repayment for saving her life.

WHEN JOHNSTON'S ARMY WAS sent to Utah to quell a rumored Mormon uprising, Colonel Albert Sydney Johnston discovered that the rebellion rumor had been greatly exaggerated, leaving him with the task of finding things for his soldiers to do.[107] Two of his men were sent to Manti, Utah, to care for a band of army horses wintering in the swamp north of town. One of the enlisted men tended to more than just the horses and got a Manti girl "into trouble." (Her reaction to his advances was not reported.) Frischknecht wrote of the incident:

> [A] *number of the town's "saints" who were skilled in the art of desexing domestic animals caught the villain and sterilized him. They nailed the organs which they had cut away to the door of the church as a warning to any amorous male who might be contemplating departure from the path*

of virtue. There were no arrests and no trials. There was no legal action. Justice had been accomplished.

Non-Mormons were not the only ones tempted to break the law of chastity.[108] When a local Manti man made the same mistake as the soldier, but with a different young lady, he went into hiding. After what he considered a sufficient cooling-off period, he resurfaced at the Sunday meeting, perhaps intent on repentance. After the "Amen"'s were said, the brother of the sullied girl spied his sister's despoiler. Taking up his gun, he shot the man dead. No legal action was taken against the shooter. Again, it was seen by the citizenry as justice served.

In a similar case that actually went to trial, the verdict was one that might take a modern-day courtroom by surprise. The tale is told in Will Bagley's column[109] of how one of Brigham Young's vanguards, Howard Egan, got away with murder.

Egan's church calling had him assisting groups from places as far-flung as California to Winter Quarters, Nebraska, to travel to Utah. Considering the methods of travel available, his calling took him away from home for lengthy periods of time. After one extended absence, he returned home to find one of his wives, Tamson Parshley Egan, with a baby that couldn't be his. He soon learned that the child's father was a traveling teacher named James Monroe who had once taught the prophet Joseph Smith's children.[110] Catching up with the seducer at Cache Caves near Logan, Utah, Egan walked up to Monroe with his revolver in hand and shot him dead in front of a wagon train of witnesses.

Egan went to trial for premeditated murder. His defense lawyer was George Albert Smith, who later became president of the Church of Jesus Christ of Latter-day Saints. Smith successfully defended his client by claiming that the laws of the federal government, which were based on old, corrupt British laws, did not apply to vigorous mountain people who were establishing a new land. Smith is credited with saying, "The man who seduces his neighbor's wife must die, and her nearest relative must kill him." He illustrated his defense with accounts of other United States citizens who had been justified in killing the seducers of wives and daughters.

Proposing that a righteous verdict would acquit Egan, he went on to compare a man who prostitutes any female to a wolf or dog killing sheep. He further declared that the chastity of women must be preserved by whatever means necessary and that the offenders must not escape for a moment. Egan was acquitted. He named the illegitimate baby William Monroe Egan and raised him as his own.

Interestingly enough, unlike some tales of slave owners seeing no lawlessness in taking sexual advantage of their slaves, it appears that preserving the chastity of women from any culture was important to some of the white men who helped settle the West. In an account by Robert D. Nielson,[111] a white man was made to account for sexually molesting an Indian maiden. Old-timers report that the accused was a married settler who was childless. After his capture, he was tried by his peers and found guilty. He was then given the penalty of "modifying his masculinity, and he sinned no more." In spite of the life-changing punishment, it is reported that he lived to an old age.

WHEN CULTURES CLASH, CRIMES against women can be hard to define. What is seen as violence in one society may be viewed as perfectly normal in another, even by the "victim." In one case, this type of cross-cultural interference had murderous consequences.[112]

On July 17, 1853, Mrs. James Ivie of Springville, Utah, traded an Indian woman some flour for three fish. Seeing how much flour his wife had, the

"Chief Walker, Isaac Morley, and wife statue." *Jacobkhed (own work), licensed under CC0 via Wikimedia Commons.*

Indian woman's dissatisfied husband began beating her for making a poor trade. James Ivie sprang to the Indian woman's defense, which escalated into battling the Indian man for possession of a gun. (The source of this information does not reveal who had the gun initially, nor what type of firearm it was.) When the gun broke, the Indian held the stock, and Ivie used the barrel in his hand to strike the Indian. The blow ended up killing the Indian man.

To Ivie's surprise, the Indian woman he'd tried to protect attacked him with such vigor that he felt he also had to strike her with the gun barrel in self-defense. It was not reported whether she lived or died. When it was all over, the local authorities knew the incident could bring dire repercussions, so they asked Chief Walkara (or Wakara, sometimes Anglicized to "Walker") for his terms of peace. He demanded that Ivie be delivered up to the tribe for an Indian trial. Springville officials rejected his decree and prepared for war, which ultimately caused the death of at least a dozen Springville settlers (Indian casualties were unreported) and the theft of hundreds of head of livestock.

Eventually, Brigham Young was successful in ending the war ten months after it began by giving the chief trinkets and tobacco and appealing to his reason.

THEFT

Taking something from someone who is trying to survive in the wilderness could be the tipping point between life and death. That might be why the crime of stealing horses was often punished by death, whether through the courts or by mob justice aided by a rope slung over the limb of a tree.

Many Native Americans seemed to hold the belief that if something belonged to you, it was only yours until they could take it. Then it belonged to them. Chief Walkara traveled across the West to the Pacific Ocean and south to Mexico.[113] When he made the acquaintance of trappers Jim Beckwourth and Pegleg Smith, they traveled to California together, intent on rounding up some fresh horseflesh to take back with them. The trappers got sidetracked and ended up trading their skins for firewater, while Walkara and his band rounded up six hundred head of horses and made a safe getaway.

Thinking that taking all the horses and deserting the trappers may have turned his friends into enemies, Walkara kept tabs on their whereabouts. He learned that Beckwourth went back to the Bear River, while Pegleg went drinking and gambling in Santa Fe saloons. In spite of his efforts to keep track of them, one day the two men rode into Walkara's camp without warning. The chief offered them food and firewater, which helped create a jovial atmosphere. In a spirit of camaraderie, they planned a large-scale horse robbery in California. The strategy was for several groups to strike simultaneously and then flee the scene of the crime along different routes.

Beckwourth took a small company of men and scouted the area for a month, studying roads, trails, watering places and the location of the best horses, all the while assuring local Spanish ranchers that he was only in search of sea lion skins.

When the strike was made, Walkara's part was to overcome the guards at the San Luis Obispo Ranch and drive off one thousand of the best horses on the continent. He and his band also made off with saddles, blankets, bridles and spurs. It is estimated that the heist from all the robberies netted the thieves three thousand horses.

While making his escape, the chief knew that his pursuers would be faster than the horses he drove ahead of him, so he and a few of his raiders lay in wait at a watering hole where they had a good view of their enemy when they set up camp. Once the posse's mounts were turned loose to graze, the horse thieves stormed into camp, shooting, whooping and driving off the horses, leaving the Californians to walk home in defeat.

On yet another occasion,[114] Walkara made his way into Old Mexico to steal more horses. The excursion was a success until the stolen horses refused to cross the rain-swollen Colorado River. When scouts warned Walkara that the Mexicans would soon catch up to them, the wily chief hid most of his men and horses in the hills before retracing his steps. When he met up with the men who were after him, he was leaning on a stolen horse's neck, feigning sickness and exhaustion. In Spanish, he told the Mexicans a sad tale about cruel Chief Walkara compelling him and others to steal against their will. The Mexicans not only believed him but also gave him a few horses and permitted him to go his way.

A NOTABLE WAR BETWEEN Indians and whites reportedly began with the crime of theft when Chief Black Hawk and his companions helped themselves to supplies from the Indian farm store in Spanish Fork, Utah, while store manager Bill Berry was away.[115] When Berry discovered the illegal shopping spree, he and Alan Durfey went in pursuit of the thieves and overtook them in Payson, Utah.

Ignoring the command to stop, Chief Black Hawk tried fitting an arrow to his bow but was hampered by his overloaded packhorse. In

The monument describes how the area near Salina, Utah, was a part of the beginnings of the Black Hawk War. *Jacobkhed (own work), licensed under CC0 via Wikimedia Commons.*

self-defense, Berry, who was unarmed, leapt off his horse and grabbed a big brass bucket that Black Hawk had taken from the store. He promptly thrust it over the chief's head, giving Payson residents time to come to the rescue. Once the goods were recovered, the Indians were released. Black Hawk left, humiliated at his treatment at the hands of the white people. He'd grown up among them and had even attended the white man's school, where he had gained much respect for his teacher, Jesse Fox.

On Sunday, April 9, 1865, Ute tribal leaders met with prominent Manti men to discuss the issue of cattle stealing. John Lowry and Archibald Buchanan acted as interpreters. Rather than try to solve the problem, Jake Arapeen seemed eager to incite the other natives to anger. Lowry finally looked up at Arapeen where he sat on his horse and told him to be quiet. A sudden shouted warning of, "Look out, he's going to shoot!" prompted Lowry to reach up and jerk Arapeen off his horse. He gave the Indian a stern lecture before releasing him.

Knowing that Black Hawk had gone to dinner at James Tooth's house after attending the white man's church, Arapeen rode to Tooth's home and told the chief his story. Too close to his own humiliation to be ignored, Black Hawk stomped out of his friend's home, determined to sever all ties with the white men he'd once called friends. His vengefulness grew into a plan to unite many tribes in warfare against the white intruders.

The war raged over the countryside, with people dying on both sides. The fighting caused the white men to lose precious time for growing critically needed crops. In spite of all his rancor, one curious incident during the war showed a keen sense of Black Hawk's personal code of Native American justice.[116] Black Hawk had promised his friend Bishop Kearns of Gunnison, Utah, that he and his family would not be harmed by the Indian people. This promise was broken during a fight in Salina Canyon on April 12, 1865, when an Indian bullet

Portraits of the Ute Indians, Chief Joseph Walker and his brother, Arapeen. *From* Route from Liverpool to Great Salt Lake Valley *(1855).*

killed the bishop's son, William. Even though the body was tucked under a rock overhang and respectfully covered by an Indian-made screen of tightly woven willow branches instead of the body being mutilated, as was the normal practice, it was not enough to compensate for a broken promise.

So, in exchange for the loss of his son, Black Hawk approached Bishop Kearns and bared his chest in a self-imposed sentence of death at the hands of his friend. Bishop Kearns refused to carry out the sentence, saying that taking another life would not bring his son back. All he asked was that Black Hawk stop the war so that they could be friends always.

Black Hawk abruptly left the warpath in 1867. Perhaps his conscience got the better of him, or he may have realized the futility of the battle or even been stopped by a personal injury he received in a skirmish. Paying a self-imposed penalty, he presented himself at the Uintah Reservation and said he wanted peace. On August 19, 1868, Black Hawk and other chiefs smoked a peace pipe with white leaders, including Orson Hyde. Although fringe outlaws continued sporadic ambushes until 1892, the war was officially over.

Left: Another monument noting the part the area around Salina, Utah, played in the Black Hawk War. *Jacobkhed (own work), licensed under CC0 via Wikimedia Commons.*

Below: Home of William Seely, the first bishop of Mount Pleasant, Utah. The Black Hawk War Treaty was signed at this residence in 1872. *Mormon Pioneer National Heritage Area.*

In an unprecedented twist, a few weeks before he died in 1870, the old chief resolved to personally seek forgiveness from every settlement where he'd caused injury. White men escorted him on his journey to both honor and protect him.

WHEN CONSIDERING SUCH DESTRUCTIOn in the aftermath of a smaller inciting incident, there were times when lesser crimes were allowed to go unpunished.[117]

Appleton "Ap" Milo Harmon was traveling with the first band of Latter-day Saints to Utah when two horses went missing. He took ten men with him and followed the horses' tracks through tall grass spreading out from a river. They soon noticed the grass moving more than it should in the slight breeze. The white men raised their rifles, which caused several Indian braves to rise up out of the grass. Even though the painted natives were armed with bows and a few rifles, they hesitated when they realized they were at the business end of the white man's firearms. Then, in friendly tones, the Indians asked for "baco."

One Indian moved close enough to shake hands and then made a grab for one of the white men's horse's reins, seemingly intent on stealing it. Certain that these Indians knew the whereabouts of the missing horses, some of the white men wanted to make them give up the horses by force if necessary, but Ap declared that they could not afford an Indian war. In his opinion, two horses were not worth the life of one man. The whites left the Indians and proceeded on their journey minus two horses.

IN OUTLAW JOE WALKER'S case, family trust was warped beyond repair over stolen livestock.[118] It began after Joe's father died, and his mother accepted Uncle Whitmore's offer to manage the Walker cattle for her and her son. Whitmore moved the combined herd to Arizona, where he was killed by Indians. His widow and sons then moved the cattle operation to Utah. After Walker's mother died, Joe went to settle up on the family cattle matter but was unpleasantly surprised to find that the Whitmores denied any relationship to him. They also spurned his claim to any cattle.

Affronted and alone, Walker joined Butch Cassidy's "Wild Bunch" gang and stole some of his cattle back from the Whitmores. Joe didn't stop there. It is reported that he took part in a gang robbery of $8,000 from the Castle Gate City payroll in 1897.

After Joe helped himself to more Whitmore cattle in 1898, a posse of nine men gave chase. They caught up to him and a cowboy named Johnny Herring at their camp so early one morning that both men were still asleep in

The Wild Bunch, 1900. *Wikimedia Commons.*

their bedrolls. Mistaking the two figures for Butch Cassidy and the Sundance Kid, who had bad reputations for shooting their way out of arrests, the posse surrounded the pair and shot the bedrolls full of holes, killing both men.

PRACTICING MEDICINE WITHOUT A LICENSE

While many people in the olden days made their own poultices and cures for a variety of ailments, one woman was accused of the crime of poisoning a baby.[119] Eunice Brown and James "Polly" Brown's daughter told the following story to her granddaughter Ruth Scow.[120]

After Dr. Richards set up practice in Manti in the 1850s, an Indian warrior named Brockley despaired of Indian methods to cure his papoose of measles, so he went to Dr. Richards's office for a white man's cure. Trying to run things alone while the doctor was away, Mrs. Richards used her knowledge of her husband's practice to choose a vial of mild medicine for the Indian to give his child. Yet when Brockley administered it to his son, he thought he saw the child's toes turn a different color and bend upward at an unnatural angle.

Certain that his son was dying from poisoned medicine, Brockley grabbed a knife and dashed from his teepee, determined to carry out the "eye for an eye" code of justice on the white woman who'd given it to him. Hearing the angry Indian's yell amid the sudden commotion, Mrs. Richards ran for her life, exiting her house as Brockley entered from the other side. Then she dodged through town with Brockley in pursuit.

At last she reached the James "Polly" Brown cabin, built by a man who had adopted his mother's maiden name so he wouldn't be mistaken for the many other James Browns in his family tree. James's startled wife looked up from where she sat peeling potatoes. "Save me, save me!" Mrs. Richards gasped.

Mrs. Brown scanned the room quickly before tucking Mrs. Richards in the small space behind the open door of the brand-new lean-to built onto the house. Then Mrs. Brown scooted her chair in front of the door and sat down with her potato and peeler just as Brockley burst into the cabin. "Where is she, the white woman?" he demanded, using his knife to push aside the clothes hanging from pegs in the wall. After looking beneath the bed, he glared at Mrs. Brown. Bound by her conscience to be truthful, Mrs. Brown raised her hand toward the door without saying a word. The enraged Indian charged through the doorway without looking behind the door and exited the other side of the lean-to still in search of his victim.

As the sun went down, Brockley stopped searching the willows along the creek and returned to his teepee, where he found his child much improved.

MAIMING

While harming another person is against the law in many cultures, there are usually extenuating circumstances that may excuse this behavior. For example, if someone tries to harm a person first, the intended victim may lay claim to self-defense in fighting back. If someone threatens an innocent person, such as a child, a protector may be within his or her rights to take violent action against the perpetrator.

Rose McIff tells the story of a pioneer mother named Nancy Jane Kenner who set up house with her husband, Dr. Samuel T. Kenner, in a town located just west of Sterling, Utah, called Pettyville, a place that no longer exists.[121]

One day, while the townsmen were out hunting and the women and children were home, an Indian chief and his braves rode in on their horses and circled Nancy's house. Aware of the Native Americans' tendency to kidnap children, Nancy quickly hid hers out of sight of anyone looking in the windows. She pulled the latchstring in through the hole in the door so that no one outside could pull on it to lift the wooden bar that held the door shut. Finally, she armed herself with a butcher knife just in time to see a brown finger slide through the latchstring hole. Terrified, she watched it feel its way around as if searching for a way to open the door. Glancing at her children's hiding places, she decided that whatever it took, she had to save them. Closing her eyes, she swung the knife down toward the finger.

One loud yelp sounded through the door, followed by the noise of galloping hooves as the Indians rode away. Breathing hard, Nancy glimpsed a brown, bloody finger lying on the floor and promptly fainted.

The next morning, Dr. Kenner was home with his family when Nancy looked out the window, horrified to see the Indians riding back. This time, they didn't form a circle. Instead they dismounted, walked up to the door, and knocked. Dr. Kenner cautiously opened the door, but instead of the trouble he expected, he was greeted by requests to see the "heap brave squaw that would dare cut off finger of chief." Reluctantly, Nancy came forward to receive the praise of each Indian, who took a turn to tell her, "Heap brave squaw." The account does not mention if the nine-fingered chief was one of the party.

Spying

Dorothy Buchanan retells a story told by her grandmother[122] about an Indian named Calico Bill. He most likely got his name from his frequent visits to Mount Pleasant, Utah, where his first stop was usually the general store, where he'd buy a piece of calico cloth. Then he made his way out of town by walking past the corrals and stockyards.

After a time, residents noticed a pattern of livestock raids following Calico Bill's visits. Determining that he was a spy for his tribe, giving them information that helped them steal animals the pioneers depended on for their survival, some townsfolk determined to meet Calico Bill the next time he came to town.

Stopping him before he could buy his customary piece of cloth, they turned him around and escorted him out of city limits and into the foothills, beyond sight of town. When the men returned, it was without Calico Bill. He was never seen again.

MURDER

What one culture sees as murder, another culture might view as an act of bravery or even sport. The Indians who killed Eunice Warner Snow's husband did not seem to feel a sense of wrongdoing when they visited her house after their bloody deed. She shared her experience in a talk given in Provo, Utah, titled, "A Short Accounting of Troubles and Trials with the Indians."[123] While the speaking event took place in August, the year is not given, yet it must have been before Eunice's death in 1914.

She tells of how the "troublesome" Indians answered the accusation of stealing cattle with the argument that it was as much their right to take cattle

A monument to remember the first settlers killed by Indians in Manti, Utah, in 1853. Previously, there was a gristmill near this location. *Jacobkhed (own work), licensed under CC0 via Wikimedia Commons.*

without consent as it was for the whites to live on Indian land without consent. (Some accounts claim that the pioneers were invited to settle the Sanpete Valley by Chief Walkara in June 1849,[124] but that was not mentioned in Eunice's account.)

Butchering cattle became the lesser of two evils when Native Americans killed Eunice's husband, miller John A. Warner, at the gristmill in the mouth of Manti Canyon on October 4, 1853. Eunice later learned that John had fought desperately, managing to kill one Indian before dying.

Rather than hide their deed, the Indians visited Eunice to show off their trophies, flaunting her husband's necktie dangling around one of their necks, his pocket ruler and his pocketknife broken into the separate pieces of blade, ear spoon and button hook. Their evident joy of conquest created such anger in Eunice that to keep her from attacking the Indians herself, her father had to carry her out. Their laughter rang in her ears as she was shut in her room.

Later, a young Indian warrior received a measure of justice from Eunice for his part in the crime when he came to her house and demanded bread. She refused, but he wouldn't leave. Temper flaring, she laid her baby on the bed and "took a piece of wood that held the window up...he laughed at first...I wore that piece of wood out on him."

The Indian ran howling to the teepee village set up within sight of the fort. After telling his pitiful story to Chief Arropeen Ollie, the chief listened to Eunice's version of events. The verdict was that the young Indian brave was thenceforth referred to as "squaw."

WHILE KILLING A WHITE man fierce enough to take out one of their own was apparently seen as worthy sport, Native Americans had a sense of revenge when tribesmen were killed under specific circumstances. Some reports say that Captain Gunnison died as retaliation for Pahvant chief Moshaquop's father being murdered at the hands of California-bound Missourians. Others say it was an offshoot of the Walker War, which was taking place farther north in Springville, Utah, when the incident happened.[125]

Whatever the reason, Captain John W. Gunnison, reported as placid by nature, was killed by Indians the morning of October 26, 1853. In spite of the Indian unrest, he'd chosen not to winter over in Fillmore, Utah. Instead, he was camped near the head of the Sevier River, intent on completing more of his survey of lands west of the Mississippi River to the Pacific Ocean for a railroad. He intended to winter over in Salt Lake City, but he never made it. Seven men died with him.

Even though Captain Gunnison lost his life, he found a measure of immortality in a town named Gunnison, located just a few miles from where he died.

EVEN NATIVE AMERICANS WERE made to answer for killing one of their own, as illustrated in a story that Blodwen P. Olsen's grandmother told her.[126] When an Indian was murdered near Toquerville, Utah, and the white authorities did nothing about it, the Indians decided to hold their own council. Thirty braves sat in a circle. Without speaking out of turn or interrupting one another, each gave his opinion on who the murderer was. A few days later, the man named as the guilty one disappeared and was never seen or heard from again.

ANDREW BJERREGAARD GREW UP in Utah during a time of tension between settlers and Indians, yet his demise came not from the Native Americans but from one of his own race.[127] He'd made a life for himself since the age of six, when his disillusioned parents left him in Utah with another family while they trekked back across the plains to Missouri. No one seems to know why he was abandoned, but when Andrew eventually traveled to the Midwest to visit his aged parents, his mother said, "Oh, it's Andrew!" They apparently had a happy reunion.

In spite of being a non-member of the dominant Church of Jesus Christ of Latter-day Saints, Andrew became a prominent figure in Ephraim, Utah, ultimately serving as president of the Bank of Ephraim. When a local drunken "sport" once told Bjerregaard that he should loosen up, spend money and have a good time with silver dollars that were made to roll, Bjerregaard answered, "Like hell they are, they are made flat to stack up."

Andrew was a spry eighty-one-year-old bank president when he argued with a man identified only as "Draper." Disapproving of Draper courting his daughter, Andrew forbade him to ever contact her again. Whether he did it for love or money, Draper was convicted of entering Bjerregaard's home late one night and killing him with a stick of wood. Draper then attempted to burn the body. For his crime, he received a life sentence for murder. Amazingly enough, just six years later, his name came up for parole. Bjerregaard's family protested, but their efforts only delayed Draper being set free for three more years. Once Draper was paroled, his freedom was short-lived. In a case of poetic justice, he became the victim of a fatal burning.

WHILE CONFLICTS BETWEEN WHITE men and Native Americans dominated the early years of settling the West, an account of crime and punishment involving a black man occurred in 1925.[128]

While former Sanpete County sheriff Milton Burns served as town marshal for Castle Gate, Utah, now a ghost town, he noticed a black man named Robert Marshall wearing a gun and "looking around" the post office. With no definitive reason reported for the action, Burns took Marshall's gun. Two weeks later, a couple of boys witnessed Marshall approach Sheriff Burns on a bridge near town. The sheriff reportedly said, "Hi. What are you doing out this way?" In answer, Marshall pulled out a pistol and fired two shots into Burns. As Burns tumbled to the ground, Marshall fired three more times, kicked Burns, struck him with the butt of his pistol and shouted, "Take that, Whitie!" Before leaving the scene, Marshall took Burns's gun, $40 in currency and a $100 money order payable to the North Sanpete Bank of Utah. The boys ran for help. Burns was taken to the Castle Gate Hospital, where he died of his injuries.

Reward posters went up all around town asking for help in apprehending the suspect. Three days later, a black man named Gray reported that Marshall was sleeping in his shack north of Castle Gate. After Marshall was taken into custody, a posse of angry citizens stormed the jail and transported the prisoner to a stand of large Cottonwood trees outside Price, Utah. A mob of eight hundred to one thousand people, some with picnic baskets, watched as Robert Marshall was illegally hanged. When his body was cut down, he miraculously revived. Rather than seeing this unexpected recovery as a divine pardon, the mob proceeded to hang him again. This time, he was pronounced dead.

District Attorney Fred W. Keller, a Manti native who relocated to Monticello, was appointed by the governor as prosecuting attorney for the State of Utah. Although eleven prominent Carbon County men were indicted, they each pled "not guilty." After thirteen days of trial, all charges were eventually dropped due to lack of evidence. Enraged by the hypocrisy he saw, Judge Keller made the following statement:

> *The past thirteen days this court has called 125 witnesses. How can these people who testified demand others to uphold the laws of the Untied States of America, to give equal justice to all races, live next to and around the men involved in the lynching? They can't help but think about these men moving about free as a bird after having committed an act which is even unlawful in the eyes of God…I am ashamed at the disgraceful mockery of*

the law and order which has resulted in the affair right from the beginning, and the manner in which the State has been held up to ridicule. May God have pity on you.

Although laws may differ between eras and cultures, there appears to be an innate sense within each individual of what is honorable and right. While there will always be those who try to get away with committing crimes for their own benefit, just as there will be ones who bypass established law in an attempt to dole out justice as they see fit, if man has a working conscience, has anyone truly gotten away with anything?

Shirley thanks Bob and Andy Bahlmann and Steven J. Clark for their invaluable proofreading skills.

NOTES

CHAPTER 1

1. Raymond S. Jones, "Last Wagon through the Hole-in-the-Rock," *Desert Magazine* (June 1954): 23–25.
2. Charles Redd, "Short Cut to San Juan," *1949 Brand Book*, 1950, 7, as recorded in David E. Miller, *Hole-in-the-Rock: An Epic in the Colonization of the Great American West* (Salt Lake City: University of Utah Press, 1959), 37.
3. Miller, *Hole-in-the-Rock*, 40.
4. Melvina Duke Collett, "The San Juan Mission," unpublished family history, as recorded in Miller, *Hole-in-the-Rock*, 38.
5. Kumen Jones, "General Move to the San Juan Mission," *Notes on the San Juan Mission* journal, paragraph 4, Hole-in-the-Rock Foundation website, http://www.hirf.org.
6. Ibid., paragraph 8.
7. Platte Lyman, *Hole-in-the-Rock Journey* journal, Monday, December 1, 1879, Hole-in-the-Rock Foundation website, http://www.hirf.org.
8. Ibid., Wednesday, December 3, 1879.
9. Jones, "Times When Failure Stared Pioneers in the Face," *Notes*, paragraph 6.
10. Cornelius I. Decker, "Sketch of My Life," as recorded in Miller, *Hole-in-the-Rock*, 193.
11. Miller, *Hole-in-the-Rock*, 110.
12. Elizabeth Morris Decker, "Letter Written at Grey Mesa, February 22, 1880," as recorded in Miller, *Hole-in-the-Rock*, 197.
13. Redd, "Short Cut to San Juan," 23–24, as recorded in Miller, *Hole-in-the-Rock*, 138.
14. Miller, *Hole-in-the-Rock*, 48.

Chapter 2

15. Kathy Weisler, "White Cliffs Lost Gold Ledge in Utah," Legends of America, 2013, http://www.legendsofamerica.com/ut-lostgoldledge.html.

16. Ibid. The Weisler account notes that Rogers was wounded, while an article in the *Southern Utah News* reports that Sharp was the one wounded, Southern Utah Vacation in Kanab, "Legend of Three Lakes," taken from *Southern Utah News*, June 27, 1990, www.southernutahcondo.com/Home/three-lakes.

17. Utah Treasure, "Johnson Canyon," 2010, http://utahtreasure.blogspot.com/2010/12/johnson-canyon.html. This blog article cites the *Southern Utah News*, June 27, 1990, as one of its sources.

18. Ibid.

19. Wikipedia, "Moqui Cave," www.en.wikipedia.org/wiki/moqui_cave. The name comes from the Moqui (or Moki), which some archaeologists believe to be an ancient tribe from the Fremont or early Anasazi civilizations at an unknown period. They are not attested historically as an identifiable tribe. The name has been used by people locally to simply refer to ancient peoples of the area.

20. Celeste Tholen Rosenlof, "Filmmakers Search for Montezuma's Treasure in Kanab Pond," 2014, www.KSL.com.

21. Utah Treasure, "Johnson Canyon."

22. Ibid.

23. Southern Utah Vacation in Kanab, "Legend of Three Lakes."

Chapter 3

24. Eileen Hallet Stone, *A Homeland in the West: Utah Jews Remember* (Salt Lake City: University of Utah Press, 2001), 189–212; Eileen Hallet Stone, *Hidden History of Utah* (Charleston, SC: The History Press, 2013), 90–91.

25. Benjamin Brown (born Benjamin Lipshitz in 1885) immigrated to America in 1900. His unpublished memoirs may be found in Robert Goldberg's papers on Clarion, Special Collections, Marriott Library, University of Utah.

26. Robert Alan Goldberg, author of *Back to the Soil: The Jewish Farmers of Clarion, Utah, and Their World* (Salt Lake City: University of Utah Press, 1986), spoke to a confirmation class taught by the author on May 6, 1995. Goldberg's talk is combined with quotations selected from his publication.

27. Harry Bernstein's commentary on his father's experience in Clarion is from the unpublished Bernstein memoirs, 1984, Goldberg Papers.

28. Moshe Melamed's reflections on early Clarion are from his unpublished diary, translated from Yiddish by Adah Fogel, 1912, Goldberg Papers.

29. Isaac Friedlander's excerpts are from *Virgin Soil*, a circa 1930s monograph translated from Yiddish by Louis C. Zucker and edited by Michael T. Walton, Goldberg Papers.

30. Michael Bernstein's talk on Clarion, donated by the late Davida Bernstein Goldberg, 2000, author's collection.

CHAPTER 4

31. The author is indebted to the Redd Center at Brigham Young University for funding this project and to Westminster College and Wasatch Academy for opening their research collections to him. The author must also give a nod to Donna Glidewell, who inspired him to pursue this project. Her book tells the story of Wasatch Academy's history, but in her words, the "narrative is not complete." Donna J. Glidewell, *It Endures Like the Wasatch Mountains: The History of Wasatch Academy* (N.p.: First Book Library, 2003), iv.

32. R. Douglas Brackenridge, "Duncan James McMillan: Missionary to the Mormons," in *Fetschrift for Charles Speel*, edited by Thomas Sienkewicz (Monmouth, NJ: Monmouth College Publication, 1996).

33. *Daily Tribune*, "Presbyterian Work," [January 1, 1881], clipping, Box MSS-020, "Presbyterians and [the] Mormons Scrapbook, 1880–1906" [alternate title: R.G. McNiece, G.W. Martin and N.E. Clemson clippings], Westminster College Archives; F.C. Jensen, "Early History of Wasatch Academy," n.d., Box 06 05, "Duncan McMillan Biographical and Early Work," Wasatch Academy Museum, Mount Pleasant, Utah.

34. In 1850, the Mormon territory of Deseret was renamed the Utah territory. Technically speaking, although it was not yet a state when McMillan traveled to Mount Pleasant, he was in Utah not Deseret, but the alliteration sounded better. For the eponymous quote, see Glidewell, *It Endures Like the Wasatch Mountains*. This is where the title of her books comes from, and she speaks to this quote throughout her book: "Let it endure like the Wasatch Mountains, call it Wasatch Academy."

35. See the *Tribune* clipping, "Presbyterian Work." For discussion of McMillan's venture south from Salt Lake, see pages 12–14. For McMillan's personal account of the journey, see Duncan J. McMillan, "Pioneer Bearers of the Cross," *Home Mission Monthly* 35 (December 1920): 29.

36. Carl Wankier, "History of Presbyterian Schools in Utah," Master of Science thesis, University of Utah, 1968, 94. The Liberal Society of Mount Pleasant took its name and its purpose from the larger Liberal Party of Utah based in Salt Lake City. Both groups began in the 1870s in opposition to the Mormon Church and church rule.

37. Wankier, "History of Presbyterian Schools in Utah," abstract, 95; Mark T. Banker, *Presbyterian Missions and Cultural Interaction in the Far Southwest, 1850–1950* (Urbana: University of Illinois Press, 1993), 59; Theodore D. Martin, *Presbyterian Work in Utah*, part 3 (Salt Lake City, UT: Wheelright Lithographing Company, 1971), 278–79.

38. Dyann Dyer, "The History of Wasatch Academy," April 1962, Box 23, Wasatch Academy Museum, Mount Pleasant, Utah, page 2. See also the *Tribune* clipping, "Presbyterian Work."

39. Linda Simons, "The Splendid Work: Duncan J. McMillan in Utah," n.d., Box 23, Wasatch Academy Museum, Mount Pleasant, Utah, page 3.

40. Simons, "Splendid Work," 10; letter, Duncan McMillan to Mrs. Wall, n.d., Box 06 05, "Duncan McMillan Biographical and Early Work," Wasatch Academy Museum, Mount Pleasant, Utah.

41. Martin, *Presbyterian Work in Utah*, 275; Samuel E. Wishard, *The Mormons* (New York: Presbyterian Home Missions, 1904), 28; Martin, *Presbyterian Work in Utah*, 276; Wankier, "History of Presbyterian Schools in Utah," 6.

42. "Historical Documents by Dyer Glidwell Wankier," chapter 2, "Beginning of Church and School," Wasatch Academy Museum, Mount Pleasant, Utah.

43. Wishard, *The Mormons*, 276.

44. Martin, *Presbyterian Work in Utah*, 287–88.

45. Ibid.

46. *Daily Tribune*, "Presbyterian Work." For a more detailed analysis of the tension, see R. Douglas Brackenridge, "'Are You that Damned Presbyterian Devil?' The Evolution of an Anti-Mormon Story," *Journal of Mormon History* (Spring 1995): 80–105.

47. Martin, *Presbyterian Work in Utah*, 287. For a more detailed analysis of the tension, see Brackenridge, "'Are You that Damned Presbyterian Devil?'" Brackenridge has more corroborating sources, but the initial source is Sheldon Jackson, "Persecutions on a Home Mission Field," *Rocky Mountain Presbyterian*, April 1876, 2.

48. For the letter to his mother, see Wankier, "History of Presbyterian Schools in Utah," 95. The plumage quote is also found in Simons, "Splendid Work," 9. For the Mormon admission of Young's actions, see Brackenridge, "Duncan James McMillan."

49. *Daily Tribune*, "It's All a Lie!" March 14, 1880, Box MSS-020, "Presbyterians and [the] Mormons Scrapbook, 1880–1906."

50. *Daily Tribune*, "Rebellion in Zion," March 6, 1880, Box MSS-020, "Presbyterians and [the] Mormons Scrapbook, 1880–1906."

51. Charles W. Penrose, editor, "Fathering Falsehoods," *Deseret News*, September 17, 1881, Box MSS-020, "Presbyterians and [the] Mormons Scrapbook, 1880–1906."

52. *Daily Tribune*, "About Mission Schools," March 31, 1880, Box MSS-020, "Presbyterians and [the] Mormons Scrapbook, 1880–1906."

53. Wankier, "History of Presbyterian Schools in Utah"; *New York Herald Tribune*, "D.J. McMillan Dies; Civil War Veteran Was 93," June 28, 1939, 1.

CHAPTER 5

54. Criminal Court trial transcript, Seventh Judicial District, Price, Utah, *State of Utah v. Hiram Bebee*, Case No. 687, 505–6.

55. Utah Supreme Court decision, December 18, 1946, *State v. BeBee*, No. 6955, 175 P.2d 478. Justice Wade wrote the opinion with Justices Larson, C.J., McDonough, Pratt and Wolfe concurring.

56. Part of his answer I have taken for the title of this article.

57. Criminal Court trial transcript, 498.

58. Ibid., 499.

59. On appeal to the Board of Pardons outlining his reasons for voting for commutation to life in prison, Justice James H. Wolfe wrote in his point number three of Part I, "His teachings, perhaps not understood by others who have not read so widely, are seemingly in harmony with Christian living." Part one of the report to the secretary of the Board of Pardons, no date.

60. *Salt Lake Telegram*, January 4, 1953.

CHAPTER 6

61. Dr. Joe Wheeler, "Why You Should Read Zane Grey," Zane Grey's West Society, http://zgws.org/zgwsread.php.

62. Dr. Joe Wheeler, e-mail message to author, July 3, 2007.

63. Specifically the short story "Canyon Walls."

64. Support for a Utah-Arizona Strip connection to *Riders of the Purple Sage* is provided further in this chapter. *Robbers Roost* was not about the Utah-Arizona Strip, although the location of the novel is not far away. However, Mount Trumbull is mentioned in the book.

65. Zane Grey's West Society, "A Listing of Movies Made from Zane Grey's Writings," http://zgws.org/zgmovies.php.

66. Internet Movie Database (IMDb), http://www.imdb.com.

67. Thomas H. Pauly, *Zane Grey: His Life, His Adventures, His Women* (Urbana: University of Illinois Press, 2007), 215, 256.

68. Candace C. Kant, *Dolly and Zane Grey: Letters from a Marriage* (Reno: University of Nevada Press, 2008).

69. See Pauly, *Zane Grey*, 71–94.

70. Library of Congress, "Books that Shaped America," http://www.loc.gov/exhibits/books-that-shaped-america.

71. Zane Grey, 1908 trip journal, Ms. 230, Zane Grey Collection, Cline Library, Northern Arizona University, Flagstaff, Arizona.

72. Conor Watkins and J. Davis Rogers, "Grand Canyon Research: Landsliding and Channel Blockages in Tapeat Creak," Missouri University of Science and Technology, http://web.mst.edu/~rogersda/cp_megalandslides/tapeats_creek.htm.

73. Hydro Adventures, "Thunder River Deer Creek," http://www.hydrosadventures.com/thunderriverdeercreek.html.

74. Zane Grey, *Riders of the Purple Sage* (New York: Grosset & Dunlap, 1912), 61, 63.

75. Pauly, *Zane Grey*, 84.

76. *Riders of the Purple Sage*, 15.

77. Ibid, 85.

78. National Park Service, "Application for Inclusion on the National Register of Historic Places," http://pdfhost.focus.nps.gov/docs/NRHP/Text/83003497.pdf.

79. Carolyn Grygla, Facebook message to Ed Meyer, November 15, 2014.

80. Charles G. Pfeiffer, *The Surprise Valleys of Zane Grey* (Columbia, SC: Charles G. Pfeiffer, 1990), 24.

81. Val Jackson interview with author, July 23, 2009.

82. Bob Whitaker, interview with author, December 21, 2014.

83. Roland Rider, *The Roll Away Saloon* (Logan: Utah State University Press, 1985), 59.

84. Graham St. John Stott, "Zane Grey and James Simpson Emmett," ms, BYU Studies (Provo, UT: Brigham Young University, 1978), 2–3.

85. Family Search Ancestral File, Family Group Record, "James Simpson Emmett," AFN:1FR4-3C, https://familysearch.org/ark:/61903/2:1:M7F6-74T.

86. Frederick H. Swanson, *Dave Rust: A Life in the Canyons* (Salt Lake City: University of Utah Press, 2007), 67.

87. Although White Sage is identified in this article as Kanab, there is value in noting that the ranch of Jimmy Owens, who accompanied Zane Grey on his lion hunting adventures in 1907 and 1908, is White Sage Ranch, located along Forest Road 22 east of Fredonia.

88. Zane Grey, *Heritage of the Desert* (New York: Harper and Bros., 1910), 31–49.

89. Ibid., 120–33.

90. Ibid., 215–34.

91. Grey, 1908 trip journal.

92. Kathy Brock, interview with the author, January 17, 2015.

Chapter 8

93. Lura Redd, *Biography of Hans Ulrich Bryner Jr.* (N.p., n.d.). Copy in possession of author. Lura Redd was a granddaughter of Hans Ulrich Bryner Jr. and Anna Dorothea Mathys.

94. Ibid.

95. Ibid.

96. "Hunt Wagon Train Diary," December 15, 1856 (date of last entry), LDS Archives.

97. Redd, *Biography of Hans Ulrich Bryner Jr.*

98. "Hunt Wagon Train Diary."

99. Melvin L. Bashore, "On the Heels of the Handcart Tragedy: Mormondom's Forgotten 1856 Wagon Companies." *Annals of Wyoming* 68 (Summer 1996): 38–49.

100. Redd, *Biography of Hans Ulrich Bryner Jr.*

101. Ibid.

102. Ibid.

103. Hans Ulrich Bryner Jr., *History of Hans Ulrich Bryner.* Copy in possession of author. The work is written in rhyme. This history was written by Ulrich on his seventy-fifth birthday, three years prior to his death.

104. Redd, *Biography of Hans Ulrich Bryner Jr.*

CHAPTER 9

105. Conrad Frischknecht, "Pioneer Justice," *Saga of the Sanpitch*, vol. 15, 1st ed. (Salina, UT: Valley Printing, 1983), 17–18.

106. Jewel K. Larsen, "An Anecdote (King Family)," *Saga of the Sanpitch*, vol. 12, 1st ed. (Manti, UT: Manti Region Church of Jesus Christ of Latter-day Saints, 1980), 1.

107. Frischknecht, "Pioneer Justice," 16–17.

108. Ibid., 17.

109. Will Bagley, "Utah History to Go," *Salt Lake Tribune*, September 17, 2000.

110. Miss Stace, "Howard and Tamson Egan," *Who We Are and Where We Came From: Howard and Tamson Egan*, Blogspot, May 16, 2011.

111. Robert D. Nielson, "Settlement of Sanpitch River Basin," *Saga of the Sanpitch*, vol. 30, 1st ed. (Ephraim, UT: Sanpete Historical Writing Committee, 1998), 128.

112. Conrad Frischknecht, "Walkara," *Saga of the Sanpitch*, vol. 20, 1st ed. (Manti, UT: Sanpete Historical Writing Committee, 1998), 80–81.

113. Ibid., 74–75.

114. Ibid., 75.

115. Virginia K. Nielson, "Black Hawk and His War," *Saga of the Sanpitch*, vol. 12, 1st ed. (Manti, UT: Manti Region of the Church of Jesus Christ of Latter-day Saints, 1980), 81–83.

116. Janell Harris, "Black Hawk's Promise," *Saga of the Sanpitch*, vol. 3, 1st ed. (Manti, UT: Manti Region of the Church of Jesus Christ of Latter-day Saints, 1971), 27–28.

117. Blodwen P. Olsen, "The Miles," *Saga of the Sanpitch*, vol. 22, 1st ed. (Ephraim, UT: Sanpete Historical Writing Committee, 1990), 99–100.

118. The Wild West, "Wild West Outlaws and Lawmen: Joe Walker," http:// www.thewildwest.org/cowboys/wildwestoutlawsandlawmen/193-joewalker.

119. Ruth D. Scow, "The White Woman," *Saga of the Sanpitch*, vol. 16, 1st ed. (Ephraim, UT: Sanpete Historical Writing Committee, 1984), 62–63.

120. Eunice C. Herbert and Leah B. Lyman, "James Polly Brown History," Family Search, the Church of Jesus Christ of Latter-day Saints, March 28, 2013, https://familysearch.org/photos/stories/424646.

121. Rose McIff, "Heap Brave Squaw," *Saga of the Sanpitch: Silver Sunsets*, vol. 25, 1st ed. (Ephraim, UT: Sanpete Historical Writing Committee, 1993), 10.

122. Dorothy J. Buchanan, "Calico Bill," *Saga of the Sanpitch* (Manti, UT: Manti Region of the Church of Jesus Christ of Latter-day Saints, 1971), 6–7.

123. Eunice W. Snow, "A Short Accounting of Troubles and Trials with the Indians," *Saga of the Sanpitch*, vol. 29, 1st ed., compiled by Udell S. Anderson (Ephraim, UT: Sanpete Historical Writing Committee, 1997), 41–44.

124. Albert Antrei, "Manti," *Utah History Encyclopedia*, 1992, http://historytogo.utah.gov/places/manti.html.

125. Donald F. Kraack, "Captain Gunnison's Folly," *Saga of the Sanpitch*, vol. 11, 1st ed. (Manti, UT: Manti Region of the Church of Jesus Christ of Latter-day Saints, 1979), 5–8.

126. Blodwen P. Olsen, "Indians in My Life," *Saga of the Sanpitch*, vol. 28, 1st ed. (Ephraim, UT: Sanpete Historical Writing Committee, 1996), 42.

127. Donald F. Kraack, "The Dauntless Dane of Sanpete County," *Saga of the Sanpitch*, vol. 10 (Manti, UT: Manti Region of the Church of Jesus Christ of Latter-day Saints, 1978), 31+.

128. David Mackey, "History Carved on a Cellar Wall," *Saga of the Sanpitch*, vol. 16, 1st ed. (Ephraim, UT: Sanpete Historical Writing Committee, 1984), 3–4.

ABOUT THE AUTHORS

MONTE BONA

Monte Bona, director of the Mormon Pioneer National Heritage Area, is a retired businessman who is completing his twentieth year as a city council member in Mount Pleasant, Utah. A graduate of Brigham Young University and the University of Michigan, he taught political science (part time) at BYU and UVU. He was a member of the U.S. Electoral College in 1972 (Michigan). He received a Utah Heritage Foundation Award "for having a vision that utilizes historic preservation and working tirelessly throughout central Utah to save historic buildings and create the Mormon Pioneer National Heritage Area."

The Utah Division of State History presented him with an Outstanding Contribution Award "in recognition of his outstanding efforts in preserving the history of Sanpete County."

Utah's Six County Association of Governments gave him a Regional Recognition Award "in recognition of the tireless effort, resolute determination, and enduring qualities which brought about the evolutionary development of a congressional heritage area designation from a mere idea which has greatly enhanced the vitality of the Six County Region through job creation and retention."

CHRISTIAN PROBASCO

Christian Probasco is a former publicity writer for the Mormon Pioneer National Heritage Area and former managing editor of the *Sanpete Messenger* newspaper in the northern "Little Denmark" district of the MPNHA. Probasco is also the author of *Highway 12*, about scenic State Route 12, Utah's only All-American Road, from which travelers can access Bryce Canyon National Park and Capitol Reef National Park, as well as three state parks, the Grand Staircase–Escalante National Monument and the route from Escalante to Hole-in-the-Rock.

STEVEN J. CLARK

Award-winning author Steven J. Clark began his career with a short story published in his junior high school annual, *The Panther*, when he was in seventh grade. Clark later went on to a more than thirty-year career in marketing and sales. He is the former editor and publisher of a national trade journal, *Manufactured Housing News*. Clark has written extensively for local and regional newspapers.

Clark's debut full-length novel was published in February 2014 by New Horizons Press/Publishers, LLC, and is entitled *All the Pretty Dresses*. It is a breathtaking mystery thriller set in the mountains of West Virginia. In September 2014, he was awarded a top-ten finish in the prestigious Critique My Novel international book competition. Clark's second novel, *Wages of Greed*, is a heart-pounding legal thriller (Tony Hillerman meets John Grisham) set in and around the Navajo reservation in the Four Corners area. It is scheduled for publication in March 2015.

Clark resides in Sanpete County, Utah, with his wife, Lauri, a large white dog named Caspar, four cats who occasionally show up for dinner and seven chickens. He is active in Utah writing circles and in local civic organizations. He invites you to visit his website at www.stevenjclark.com and welcomes contact with readers by e-mail at sjc@cut.net.

EILEEN HALLET STONE

Transplanted from New England, Utah-based writer Eileen Hallet Stone's award-winning projects include topics such as nineteenth-century life, populations in crisis, community stories and ethnic histories. Her latest book, *Hidden History of Utah*, is a compilation of her *Salt Lake Tribune* columns. Her collected stories in *A Homeland in the West: Utah Jews Remember* were developed into a photo-documentary exhibit for the 2002 Winter Olympic Cultural Olympiad Arts Festival in Salt Lake City. *Missing Stories: An Oral History of Ethnic and Minority Groups in Utah*, co-authored with Leslie Kelen, added substantially to Utah's educational curriculum. She writes a "Living History" column for the *Salt Lake Tribune*. She has one son, Daniel, and lives with her husband, Randy Silverman, in the eclectic Sugar House area of Salt Lake City.

JASON FRIEDMAN

Raised in New York City, Jason Friedman has been working in academia for the past fourteen years. Friedman received his PhD in history from Michigan State University in 2009 and works currently as a history and political science instructor at Wasatch Academy. A modern American

historian, Friedman's primary research focuses on the cultural issues surrounding the American presidency and the balance of power during the 1970s. However, in deference to his current station in life, Friedman has expanded his historical research interests to include the institutional history of Wasatch Academy, specifically the history of the school's founder, Duncan McMillan.

JACK C. BILLINGS

Jack C. Billings is a third-generation descendant of immigrant Mormon converts. Although not a member of his ancestors' church, he remains close to his roots, residing still at the Bountiful, Utah house he was brought to as a baby. While interested in writing in high school in Boise, Idaho, and also in college at the University of Utah, he is a late arrival with this, his first piece of writing outside the occasional op-ed newspaper submission. His interest in his subject, Hiram Bebee, is direct and personal; Jack is mentioned, as a toddler, in correspondence sent from the state prison by Bebee to Jack's mother. These are ties that border on blood relationship.

ED MEYER

Ed Meyer was the original director of the Utah Heritage Highway 89 Alliance, later to become the Mormon Pioneer National Heritage Area. For three decades, he directed Utah's rural development programs as an appointee of five Utah governors. He served as a city councilman

in Kanab, Utah, where he played a leadership role in creating the Kanab Entrepreneur Forum and the Center for Education, Business and the Arts. He also served on the Kanab Arts Council and the Kanab Heritage Council. Meyer is currently a board member of Zane Grey's West Society, where is also the marketing director and content manager for its Facebook page. He recently completed *Canyon Covenants*, a historic fiction novel about James Simpson Emett, a bigger-than-life polygamist cowboy living along the Colorado River just before and after the beginning of the twentieth century. He and his wife, Kathy, currently own homes in Kanab, Utah, and Florence, Arizona.

JAMES NELSON

James Nelson is an award-winning journalist and producer of radio and television documentaries. Nelson created the ongoing TV series *Discovery Road*, which chronicles the history, culture and heritage along the Mormon Pioneer National Heritage Area (MPNHA). He also works as a reporter and producer for national and international news agencies covering high-profile court cases, breaking news, feature stories and entertainment. His clients have included *ABC World News*, *Good Morning America*, ABC News' *20/20*, PBS, NPR, Monocle radio in London, the Sundance Film Festival, the National Basketball Association, Reuters and CBS news.

JACK MONNETT

Jack Monnett holds a PhD in history from the University of Utah, where he studied Utah history and the foundations of Utah education. He has both taught and been an administrator in Latter-day Saint as well as public higher education systems and is past president of a book publishing company. He is the author of six previously published books and currently serves as the mayor of a small Utah town.

ABOUT THE AUTHORS

Shirley Bahlmann

Shirley Anderson Bahlmann was born in the West and then moved with her family to the East Coast when she was two. An avid reader, she had to hide in the closet to read books so her mother wouldn't put her to work for "not doing anything." Shirley wrote her first novel of twenty-five handwritten pages in the fifth grade.

After ten years of suburban living, her family moved back to the mountains of Utah, where Shirley met and married Bob Bahlmann. Their six sons led to her years of service in the PTA and on more than one School to Community Council.

Shirley has always been interested in old houses, the people who built them and the ones who traveled past them. Among the more than twenty books she's written is a series of true pioneer story collections, and she has another one in the works. She's taught creative writing to adults and children for more than ten years, worked as a children's librarian, chaired the LDStorymakers Writing Conference and is currently chair of the Write Here in Ephraim Conference. She's presented at various seminars and conferences and serves on the Scandinavian Festival Board for storytelling in Ephraim, Utah. Find out more about Shirley at www.shirleybahlmann.com.